ELLA HICKSON

Ella Hickson's debut ｐ
won a Fringe First Award, the Carol Tambor 'Best of
Edinburgh' Award and was nominated for an Evening Standard
Award. It transferred to the Trafalgar Studios, London, and
PS122, New York. Her other plays include *Precious Little
Talent* (Bedlam Theatre, Edinburgh and Trafalgar Studios,
London); *Hot Mess* (Hawke & Hunter, Edinburgh and Latitude
Festival); *Soup* (Òran Mór at Traverse Theatre, Edinburgh);
PMQ (Theatre 503 and HighTide Festival) and *Boys*. She
completed a creative writing MA at the University of Edinburgh
and spent a year working with the Traverse Theatre as their
Emerging Playwright on Attachment. She has taken part in the
Royal Court Invitation Group and is the Pearson Playwright in
Residence for the Lyric Hammersmith.

Ella is under commission to Headlong Theatre and Radio 4 and
is participating in Channel 4's Screenwriting Course. She is a
member of the Old Vic New Voices and has taken part in the
24 Hour Plays, Ignite and the T.S. Eliot UK/US Exchange.

Other Titles in this Series

Ella Hickson

PRECIOUS
LITTLE TALENT
&
HOT MESS

Two plays

NICK HERN BOOKS
London
www.nickhernbooks.co.uk

A Nick Hern Book

Precious Little Talent & Hot Mess first published in Great Britain as a paperback original in 2011 by Nick Hern Books Limited, 14 Larden Road, London W3 7ST

Precious Little Talent & Hot Mess copyright © 2011 Ella Hickson

Ella Hickson has asserted her right to be identified as the author of these works

Cover photograph by Idil Sukan for Draw HQ
Cover design by Ned Hoste, 2H

Typeset by Nick Hern Books, London
Printed in Great Britain by CLE Print Ltd, St Ives, Cambs PE27 3LE

A CIP catalogue record for this book is available from the British Library

ISBN   978 1 84842 166 0

PRECIOUS LITTLE TALENT

For Simon

With thanks for his optimism

'*The difficulty is that the English are finding it impossible to give any account of themselves except for identities that they are dragging up from the past. There has never been a time when some coherent account of English National Identity was more needed.*'

Krishan Kumar

'*American Democracy: a tradition based on the simple idea that we have a stake in each other and that what binds us together is greater than what drives us apart and if enough people believe in the truth of that proposition and act on it then we might not solve every problem but we can get something meaningful done.*'

Barack Obama

'*E pluribus unum*' – '*Out of the many, one.*'

Motto on an American one cent coin

Acknowledgements

I would like to thank, first and foremost the Jameses; James Dacre for his relentless energy and commitment to high standards and James Quaife for his super-human ability to make things happen at short notice. I thank them both for working round the clock, for keeping the faith and for having the tenacity and tolerance to have maintained a sense of humour when things have got tough.

I would like to thank Simon Ginty, Emma Hiddleston, John McColl, Cat Hobart, Xander Macmillan, Polly Bennett and Jessica Winch. Much of the original script was influenced by conversations with these people. I consider myself hugely lucky to have worked with such talented collaborators.

I would like to thank Katherine Mendelsohn, David Greig, Carol Tambor and Kent Lawson.

Finally, my thanks go to Jess Cooper and my family for their unfaltering support.

Ella Hickson

Precious Little Talent was first performed at the Bedlam Theatre, Edinburgh, on 6 August 2009, as part of the Edinburgh Festival Fringe, with the following cast:

SAM	Simon Ginty
JOEY	Emma Hiddleston
GEORGE	John McColl
Director	Ella Hickson
Technical Manager	Xander Macmillan
Stage Manager	Cat Hobart
Movement Director	Polly Bennett
Producer	Jess Winch for Tantrums Ltd

A revised full-length production transferred to the Trafalgar Studios, London, on 5 April 2011, with the following cast:

SAM	Anthony Welsh
JOEY	Olivia Hallinan
GEORGE	Ian Gelder
Director	James Dacre
Designer	Lucy Osborne
Lighting Designer	Mark Jonathan
Sound Designer	Emma Laxton
Producer	James Quaife for Tantrums Ltd

6

Characters

SAM, *nineteen, American*
JOEY, *twenty-three, English*
GEORGE, *sixty-one, English, Joey's father*

The play takes place in

New York, December, 2008
New York, February, 2009
London, April, 2011

This text went to press before the end of rehearsals and so may differ slightly from the play as performed.

ACT ONE

One

Late night.

Christmas Eve, 2008.

A rooftop – New York City.

SAM (*to audience*). It's Christmas Eve in the winter of two thousand eight and the night is cruel and beautiful and it feels like it's the first time it's ever been that way. I'm sitting on a rooftop, downtown New York City; in front of me midtown, pouring out into the night like a million luminous toothpicks, but right around me is black, black and death. I'm nineteen and I've got an erection, right tight into the front of my pants 'cos I can feel a woman's breath on the left side of my neck. This nervous little breath, panting, just beneath my ear; the moisture in it licking at me in the dark night and I so desperately want to turn around and suck that in, so desperately – but I keep my hands on my thighs, just like this and I say 'hey'.

JOEY. Hey.

SAM. What's your name?

JOEY. Joey.

SAM. No shit, mine too!

JOEY. Really?

SAM. No, it's Sam. I'm sorry – I don't know why I just said that.

(*To audience.*) She laughs this funny little laugh and it sounds funny so I say –

You sound funny.

JOEY. I'm English.

SAM (*to audience*). She says, all like that, all 'I'm English', like that.

(*To* JOEY.) So you're British, eh?

JOEY. No, I'm English. No one's really British. People who say they're British are just embarrassed about being English.

SAM. What about the Scots and the Irish?

JOEY. They're Scottish and Irish.

SAM. And isn't there Wales?

JOEY. Everyone sort of forgets about Wales.

SAM. Tough to be Welsh, eh?

JOEY. I guess.

Pause.

SAM. Politics makes for bad sex.

JOEY. What?

SAM. Um – sorry, it was something my dad always used to say – I – I don't know why I – um… So… you're up here for, um – a little air?

JOEY. Yep.

SAM (*to audience*). So I'm thinking 'a little air', like taking a turn on the veranda, like a midnight, moonlit stroll, like Audrey Hepburn at dawn before breakfast time at Tiffany's; like this is the moment you might tell your kids that you met and she says –

JOEY. Hepburn.

SAM. Hepburn?

JOEY. Hepburn.

SAM. How did you do that?

JOEY. I just – how old are you, Sam?

SAM. How old are you?

JOEY. Twenty-three.

SAM. No freaking way – me too!

JOEY. Really?

SAM. No, absolutely not, I'm nineteen. I'm sorry, I don't know why I – you can check my driver's license if you want.

(*To audience*.) And she only fucking does! She slides these little British, English, fingers right into my back pocket, so as I can feel the bump of her ring dig in against my butt cheek – and then BAM; I stare her right in the face, eyeball to eyeball, and that little licky breath is all over my face and my lips, all warm and moist but I don't flinch an inch... she has this pale skin and pink cheeks like she's been out in the snow...

(*To* JOEY.) Your hand is in my pocket.

JOEY. It's warm.

SAM. Okay, keep it there. That's fine by me.

(*To audience*.) And then I'm sure you won't believe this, I'm sure you will have heard this said a thousand times before but piano music starts to play. A really well-known tune, I know, but it was, I swear to you –

Beethoven's 'Moonlight Sonata' starts to play.

That's it! That's exactly the one! I swear, I swear, ladies and gentlemen, it came swinging up over the fire escapes like a beautiful baboon and fills right up all the air around us like it's smoke and ashes and she looks at me, right dead smack in the eyes. She has beautiful eyes, like two tiny tiny fires and she pokes out her little tongue all pinky in the night sky and she... licks me. Right across my top lip; and I feel like it might just be the end of the world if she leaves.

And suddenly we're running fast as our feet will take us, stamping down fire escapes, looking in on late-night offices where tired and desperate men are sitting and watching dollars dropping like flies but we're running, fast and quick and furious. We're headed down Bleeker where the lights are kind and the windows are crowded up with smart stuff and slutty stuff and it's cold, you see, so cold that my fingers get numb so as they might be tempted to let go of the very best thing that they have ever had the pleasure of holding on to –

(*To* JOEY.) You want to take the subway?

JOEY. Sure.

SAM (*to audience*). We take the uptown 6 train that goes all the way up and down Manhattan, scratching its back along the side of Central Park – we take it all the way up through Astor and Union and 59th and 96th and all the way on up to Harlem and when we get to the top we just come right back again and on our way back down we just can't stop looking at each other and we laugh and we put our hands over our faces like kids in a bathtub –

JOEY. I want to get off.

SAM. Okay.

(*To audience*.) I take her hand and I lead her off that train and I've judged my timing right because we emerge right into the middle of Grand Central Station.

Have you ever been there? Oh, I'm sure you have in movies once or twice or probably a thousand times but can I ask you to try and imagine it as if you were seeing it for exactly the first time? As if you hadn't seen a single movie, like you've never enjoyed Cary Grant running through or De Niro on his Midnight Run – imagine please that you had never even bought a picture postcard. Imagine all those chandeliers as if you had never seen a single thing twinkle in your life ever before.

And do you know what I did – right then, right in the middle of Grand Central Station? I pulled her right around and I kissed her, real hard. And when I stopped, when I stopped and stood back and I looked at her, she said the strangest thing, she said… 'I don't believe in you.'

Two

Earlier that evening.

An apartment beneath the rooftop.

TriBeCa – New York City.

SAM *and* GEORGE *are playing a game of chess.*

GEORGE. Your move.

SAM. I got nothing. I can't see what you did there.

GEORGE. I blinded you with skill.

SAM. Pretty much.

    SAM *begins to pack up the chessboard.*

GEORGE. What are you doing?

SAM. I'm packing up.

GEORGE. Why?

SAM. It's bedtime.

GEORGE. Don't be a quitter.

SAM. It's bedtime.

GEORGE. I'll decide when it's –

SAM. I got to do it before I go, George.

    SAM *goes to put a tabard on.*

GEORGE. Refill my Scotch before you go putting that thing back on.

    SAM *refills the glass.*

SAM. Anything else?

GEORGE. You could fetch me the paper but you are, no doubt, permitted to do that in your official capacity.

SAM. Tea or Ovaltine?

GEORGE. Tea.

SAM. You know, they think tea's got more caffeine in it than coffee.

GEORGE. 'They' have begun to talk nothing but bollocks. I don't want that piss-weak stuff either.

SAM. I just don't want you not to –

GEORGE (*interrupting*). Milk first! Let the milk cool the tea, don't let the tea heat the milk.

SAM. I've already put milk in there.

GEORGE. Hm.

SAM. Your blister pack's empty for today, you already taken your meds?

GEORGE. They're called pills and yes I have.

SAM. Are you sure?

GEORGE. Yes still means yes.

SAM. Okay. I ironed some clean pyjamas if you –

GEORGE. These are fine.

SAM. You've been wearing them for –

GEORGE (*interrupting*). They're fine.

SAM. You want a hand shaving?

GEORGE. No.

SAM. It's been a while since –

GEORGE (*interrupting*). I do apologise, am I offending your sensibilities, Sam?

SAM. I just thought it might be itchy.

GEORGE. Well, it's not, and if it is, I'll itch it.

SAM. Okay, I'm just going to turn your blanket on and then I'll –

GEORGE. I can flick a switch!

Beat.

SAM. George, did Marina come in this morning?

GEORGE. Yes… you know she did, I know she did, we all know she did. She wrote her name nice and large on the timetable in big pink felt-tip because, of course, I can't understand standard English letter formations unless they are the size of small countries and the colour of reconstituted flamingos.

SAM. Just checking, George.

GEORGE. And once it's written, MA-RI-NA – wipes the rest of the timetable clean as if she imagines that in that act of reading it I spray it with the various products of my various incontinences. Does she? Hm?

SAM. George?

GEORGE. Does she think that the neon letters are so cryptically befuddling to my addled brain that in a fit of confusion I violently secrete on the thing? Bafflement, confusion and consternation – I've just spat, snotted and dribbled all over this shiny timetable, I do hope – M… M–

SAM. Marina.

GEORGE. I do hope Marina is back in tomorrow to wipe it clean.

SAM. George?

GEORGE. Yes?

Beat.

SAM. She's just trying to keep things clean. She's just got habits.

GEORGE. Well she can un-habit, uninhabit my bloody kitchen and stop wiping the sodding timetable.

SAM. I'll tell her to stop wiping the timetable.

GEORGE. I'd be most obliged. (*Beat*.) Are you in tomorrow?

SAM. It's on the timeta... yeah, I'm in.

GEORGE. Why don't you have somewhere better to be?

SAM. It's double pay.

Pause.

GEORGE. What about your – uh –

SAM. Family?

GEORGE. Yes.

SAM. There are enough of them to look after each other.

GEORGE. Right, well, in which case you should probably buy a bird.

SAM. Yeah?

GEORGE. Ham sandwiches run the risk of being a little depressing.

SAM. Okay.

GEORGE. Nothing large.

SAM. You want me to bring any decorations or a cake or wear anything fancy or – I could get a tree or –

GEORGE (*interrupting*). No.

SAM. No?

GEORGE. No – business as usual; no ham.

SAM. Right. (*Beat*.) George, are you sleeping alright?

GEORGE. Yes.

SAM. Marina said she came in early this morning and you seemed a little disoriented.

GEORGE. Disorien-ta-ted.

SAM. What?

GEORGE. Disorien-ta-ted. There's an extra syllable in there, we gave you the bloody language, the least you can do is use it properly.

SAM. She said you seemed a little –

GEORGE. You can tell MA-RI-NA that I'm perfectly orientated, thank you.

SAM. I said that to her, I was just –

GEORGE (*interrupting*). I'm going to orient myself toward bed now if you don't mind.

SAM. Sure.

GEORGE. So if you'd kindly orient yourself toward leaving.

SAM. Sure, just after I've tided up.

GEORGE. It's tidy.

SAM. And then I might head up onto the roof for a smoke.

GEORGE. It's rather late, Sam.

SAM. Hell, George, it is late, it's almost Christmas Day; Merry Christmas, George.

GEORGE. Merry Christmas. (*Beat.*) Are you in tomorrow?

SAM. Sure I am.

Beat.

GEORGE. If you come to check on me I'll disembowel you.

SAM. Wouldn't dream of it.

GEORGE. You might as well have this cup of tea as well, it tastes like piss.

GEORGE *leaves the cup of tea on the side and exits.*

SAM *waits a moment, gets his coat and leaves.*

Some time passes.

GEORGE *goes into the sideboard and gets out a small gift box.*

GEORGE *opens the gift box to reveal earrings.*

GEORGE *holds them up and nervously inspects them.*

GEORGE *abandons the idea of them and puts the box back in the cupboard.*

Three

Late night.

Christmas Eve, 2008.

A rooftop – New York City.

JOEY (*to audience*). All those windows; tiny lights holding tiny lives… all in rows and columns, like a massive crossword, with none of the clues filled in yet.

SAM. Hey.

JOEY. Hey.

SAM. What's your name?

JOEY. Joey.

SAM. No shit, mine too!

JOEY. Really?

SAM. No, it's Sam. I'm sorry – I don't know why I just said that.

JOEY (*to audience*). Weird.

SAM. You sound funny.

JOEY. I'm English.

SAM. So you're British, eh?

JOEY. No, I'm English. No one's really British. People who say they're British are just embarrassed about being English.

SAM. What about the Scots and the Irish?

JOEY. They're Scottish and Irish.

SAM. And isn't there Wales?

JOEY. Everyone sort of forgets about Wales.

SAM. Tough to be Welsh, eh?

JOEY. I guess.

Pause.

SAM. Politics makes for bad sex.

JOEY. What?

(*To audience.*) What?

SAM. Um – sorry, it was something my dad always used to say – I – I don't know why I – um… So… you're up here for a little air?

JOEY. Yep. (*Burps.*) Sorry, heartburn –

SAM. Hepburn? How did you do that?

JOEY. Heartburn… the plane – food.

SAM. Oh.

JOEY. How old are you, Sam?

SAM. How old are you?

JOEY. Twenty-three.

SAM. No fucking way – me too!

JOEY. Really?

SAM. No, absolutely not, I'm nineteen. I'm sorry, I don't know why I – you can check my driver's licence if you want.

JOEY (*to audience*). Sure, why not.

JOEY *puts her hand in* SAM*'s pocket.*

SAM *snaps his head around, they lock eyes.*

SAM. Your hand is in my pocket.

JOEY. It's warm.

SAM. Okay. Keep it there. That's fine by me.

JOEY (*to audience*). And we're sitting there, stony-still, not moving a muscle and suddenly as if we were in some old-fashioned movie, my hand in his back pocket has managed to turn his iPod on and out of his earphones, right across the freezing night, comes the 'Moonlight Sonata'. Americans, what are they like?

And he's looking so sincere and earnest and he won't look away and somehow, it's too much and I just want to sort of, pop the moment and so I –

JOEY *licks* SAM *across his top lip.*

Lick him.

(*To audience.*) I grab him, and I start running. Down these fire escapes and down all these streets I've never seen before, and I keep going, you know in that way, when you're a bit drunk and you're totally convinced that you should be in the Olympics or you're Rocky or – so my feet just keep going and going and – have you ever felt that? Like you just want to run so fucking badly and nowhere is far enough? So I just keep running, faster and faster and the cold hurts my chest and my teeth ache and –

SAM *stops* JOEY.

SAM. You want to take the subway?

JOEY (*to audience*). The train feels good, the windows flashing and the faces going past – it lets you think for a second, lets you breathe. And he's still sitting there, still smiling at me, like a, I don't know... a – dog. And then the wine from the plane and the cold and the – and I think I'm going to be –

JOEY *puts her hands over her face.*

SAM *puts his hands over his face as if it's a game.*

(*To* SAM.) I want to get off.

SAM. Okay.

JOEY (*to audience*). So he grabs me and drags me through the turnstiles and up – up into the middle of Grand Central Station. People aren't lying when they say that place is beautiful. It's got the kind of grandeur that makes you feel like you can borrow a life that's better than yours, just for a moment, reminds you what fairy stories felt like – with all those chandeliers and it all beating, softly, with whispers of old movies, love affairs worth waiting for and great lines said at the right time – it makes you feel like –

SAM *grabs her and kisses her.*

I don't believe in you.

Four

It's ten o'clock in the morning.

The morning is fresh, cold and bright.

It's Christmas Day.

GEORGE *is dressed in his Sunday best.*

SAM *enters.*

SAM. Good morning, George, and a very merry –

GEORGE (*interrupting*). Please be quiet.

SAM. I didn't realise we were dressing up.

GEORGE. It's not for –

SAM. Is everything okay?

GEORGE. You need to leave.

SAM. What?

GEORGE. I don't need any help today.

SAM. You've done your buttons up wrong.

GEORGE. Did you hear me?

SAM. Yes. (*Beat.*) You look like you haven't slept.

GEORGE. Leave, please.

SAM. Why?

GEORGE. I need you to leave.

SAM. Are you okay, George?

GEORGE. Yes.

SAM. Have you taken your –

GEORGE (*interrupting*). I'm sorry but you can't stay.

SAM. I'm serious, if something has happened you need to stop being cranky and just tell me.

GEORGE. You are my employee. I am telling you to leave the premises.

Pause.

SAM. You're going to tell me or you're going to have to throw me out.

Long pause.

GEORGE. I have a guest.

SAM. You have a guest.

GEORGE. Yes.

SAM. You haven't had a guest in two years, George.

GEORGE. Well, I have a guest.

SAM. Okay. Okay –

GEORGE. Don't use that tone.

SAM. Tone?

GEORGE. Suggesting I am of unsound mind.

SAM. It wasn't a tone – I'm just saying a guest is unusual.

GEORGE. Sam, the d-defence for sanity is much the same –
p-proof for insanity so we're going to be here all bloody day
if you d-don't–

SAM. Breathe.

GEORGE. Leave.

SAM. Where is your guest, George? Show me your guest.

GEORGE. She's sleeping.

SAM. Yeah?

GEORGE. Yes.

Pause.

SAM. Oh. (*Beat.*) Wow.

GEORGE. 'Wow'?

SAM. She must have got here pretty late if I missed her?

GEORGE. She did, rather, yes. I'm not sure what this has to do
with –

SAM. It's not very wholesome, it being Christmas and all.

GEORGE. What?

SAM. She a whore?

GEORGE. No, she bloody well is not!

SAM. Sorry, that was way out of line.

GEORGE. Yes, it was.

SAM. You need me to leave.

GEORGE. Yes!

JOEY *enters in her pyjamas, rubbing her eyes.*

JOEY. Morning. Happy Chr–

JOEY *spots* SAM.

Pause.

GEORGE. Morning. Would you like a cup of tea?

JOEY. Yes; please.

SAM. Hey.

JOEY. Hey.

GEORGE. This is Sam.

JOEY. Hello, Sam.

SAM. I'll get it, the tea.

JOEY. He knows where the kettle is?

SAM. Yes.

JOEY. Right.

GEORGE. Did you sleep well?

JOEY. No, not very, jet lag.

SAM. Valerian.

JOEY. Sorry?

SAM. Valerian tea, for jet lag, works like a dream. Merry Christmas, by the way, I forgot to say… just then.

GEORGE. Tea would be lovely.

SAM *leaves to make tea.*

It'll wear off.

JOEY. What?

GEORGE. Jet lag.

JOEY. How long has he been here?

GEORGE. Sam?

JOEY. Yes.

GEORGE. Here?

JOEY. Yes.

GEORGE. Oh – not long.

SAM (*from off*). Sugar?

GEORGE *and* JOEY. No.

JOEY. It looks different in daylight.

GEORGE. It's a little –

JOEY. I should get changed. Do you know him?

GEORGE. Yes.

JOEY. Right.

GEORGE. If you're going to have a shower I'll need to turn
    the –

JOEY. He's your… neighbour?

    Beat.

GEORGE. Yes.

    SAM *enters with tea.*

SAM. Here we go – one for George and one for Joey.

JOEY. Thank you.

GEORGE. Joey?

JOEY. Yes?

GEORGE. Joanna.

SAM. Milk, Joanna?

JOEY. Thank you.

SAM. George?

GEORGE. Yes. Thank you.

JOEY. Do you know what, I should – uh, have a shower and get ready, um –

SAM (*interrupting*). Second on the left, on the way back toward the bedroom.

GEORGE. We'll put some breakfast on.

JOEY. So you'll still be here when –

SAM (*interrupting*). Oh, I don't know.

GEORGE. Off you go, Joanna.

JOEY. Right.

    JOEY *exits*.

    Pause.

GEORGE. Unusually good cup of tea, Sam.

SAM. Thanks.

GEORGE. What's the plan for lunch?

SAM. Lunch?

GEORGE. Yes.

SAM. You're shaking, George.

GEORGE. No.

SAM. Sit down.

GEORGE. Yes. Thank you.

SAM. I'll get some breakfast.

    SAM *goes to put his tabard on*.

GEORGE. Don't.

SAM. What?

GEORGE. Don't put that on. Could you put it in the drawer, please?

SAM. Sure.

GEORGE. Sam?

SAM. Yeah?

GEORGE. She can't – um – she can't know anything. It's… vital.

SAM. George, that's going to be –

GEORGE (*interrupting*). Not a thing.

SAM. Right.

GEORGE. I'm sorry for asking you to leave, it's rather complicated.

SAM. I bet it is.

GEORGE. We should have eggs, for breakfast, she likes them a certain way, I can't – I can't – um –

SAM. Scrambled, poached or boiled?

GEORGE. Scr– could I get a whisky?

SAM. It's ten o'clock in the morning.

GEORGE. Yes.

SAM. Scrambled, poached or boiled, George?

GEORGE. Sam, are you –?

SAM. Scrambled, poached or boiled – eggs?

GEORGE. Could you pass me my – my –

SAM (*interrupting*). I know it's not my place but she's very young, she's clearly in some kind of trouble and I don't think that this, you, are the right –

GEORGE (*interrupting*). What do you mean, she's in trouble?

SAM. I – um – I met her, last night and she was kind of, you know, a bit messed up, like just – lost, I guess, and I don't think her ending up here, with a man that is like three times her age, is going to do her any good.

Beat.

GEORGE. She's my daughter.

Beat.

SAM. Oh. (*Beat.*) Shit.

GEORGE. Last night?

JOEY *enters behind* SAM. SAM *doesn't see her.*

SAM. Two years and you never say you have a daughter?

JOEY. Oh.

GEORGE. Joanna, I –

JOEY (*interrupting*). Sam, it is Sam, isn't it?

SAM. Yes.

JOEY. Could you turn that up a second?

SAM. This.

JOEY. Yes. I think it's the Queen's Speech.

SAM *turns the radio up.*

(*Taunting.*) We used to listen to it when I was small, we'd have dinner, eat so much we all felt like we were going to be sick and right before we all fell asleep you'd make us sit down and listen to it, didn't you, Dad?

GEORGE. Yes.

JOEY. Why don't I go and put some breakfast on?

GEORGE. Joanna?

JOEY. Everyone okay with poached eggs?

SAM. Sounds great.

JOEY. Good.

GEORGE. Joanna?

JOEY. Your buttons are done up wrong, Dad.

JOEY exits.

Pause.

GEORGE *starts furiously trying to undo and redo his buttons and he can't manage it.*

SAM *watches for several seconds.*

SAM *goes over and helps* GEORGE.

GEORGE *rejects the help.*

GEORGE. I need to go and get some things for lunch.

SAM. I'll go.

GEORGE. No, I need the a –

SAM. I can't let you go on your own, George.

GEORGE. Keep your voice down. I am a grown man, I am going to –

SAM (*interrupting*). I can't let you do that.

GEORGE. You can't stop me.

SAM. I'll come with you.

GEORGE. I don't want her here on her own, she'll find things. You'll stay here.

GEORGE *goes to leave.*

SAM *steps in his way.*

SAM. George, I can't let you go out there on your –

JOEY enters.

JOEY. Tea or coffee?

GEORGE. I'm just going to pop out for a minute, get some bits and pieces.

JOEY. I'm doing eggs.

SAM. George?

GEORGE. Sam can help you.

JOEY. I don't need any help.

GEORGE. I won't be long.

GEORGE *exits*.

QUEEN'S VOICE (*from radio*).'Christmas is a time for celebration, but this year it is a more sombre occasion for many. Some of those things which could have been taken for granted suddenly seem less certain and, naturally, give rise to feelings of insecurity. When life seems hard, the courageous do not lie down and accept defeat; instead, they are all the more determined to struggle for a better future.

– I think we have a huge amount to learn from individuals such as these. And what I believe many of us share with them is a source of strength and peace of mind in our own families.'

End of Act One.

ACT TWO

One

JOEY *is dressed for Christmas Day. She has made an effort.*

It is midday.

JOEY *is looking for something in the sitting room, rifling through books and drawers, keeping an eye/ear out for people coming in.*

SAM *enters.*

SAM. What are you looking for?

JOEY. Where's Dad?

SAM. I don't think he's in there. (*Beat.*) You look nice.

JOEY. Thanks.

SAM. You want a drink?

JOEY. No. Thank you.

SAM. Okay. Well, I'll be in the kitchen if you –

JOEY. How come you're not with your family?

SAM. Can't afford the trip home.

JOEY. Where do they live?

SAM. Norfolk.

JOEY. What?

SAM. Norfolk, Virginia – it's just north of Portsmouth.

JOEY. Portsmouth?

SAM. It's like seven hours south, by car. What were you looking for?

JOEY *holds up a framed photograph.*

JOEY. Who are these guys?

SAM. The Romeos.

JOEY. The who?

SAM. Romeos – Retired Old Men Eating Out. It's a bunch of old British guys; he has lunch with them once a week or so.

JOEY. You live next door, don't you?

SAM. No, I live in Hoboken.

JOEY. Oh. Dad said –

SAM. Oh, sure – yeah – my aunt lives in the building.

JOEY. Right.

SAM. He never lets me in his room.

Beat.

JOEY. Okay.

SAM. What I mean is, whatever it is you're looking for – it might be in there.

JOEY. I wasn't looking for anything.

SAM. Okay. Well if you do want a drink, shout.

SAM *goes to exit.*

JOEY. Sam?

SAM. Yeah?

JOEY. Is this the only photo in the apartment?

SAM. I think so.

JOEY. No others, not lying around or in his wallet or – ?

SAM (*interrupting*). He got given that; I doubt he even knows it's there.

JOEY. There aren't any books.

SAM. He reads newspapers and magazines mostly.

JOEY. I had the smallest room in the house until I was thirteen because he refused to give up his bloody library.

SAM. You seem kind of angry.

JOEY. Have you ever considered being a psychologist, Sam?

SAM. Sure.

JOEY. Why are you here?

SAM. Why are you here?

JOEY. I asked you first.

SAM. I was here first.

JOEY. To see my dad.

SAM. Ditto.

JOEY. Are you his – cleaner?

SAM. No.

JOEY. His cook, his student, his –

SAM. I'm his friend.

JOEY. You're nineteen.

SAM. You want to check my –

JOEY. No.

SAM. I come say 'hey' every now and then, we hang out, we play chess, we talk, we watch movies – I just come say 'hey'. No one else does.

JOEY. Meaning?

SAM. Nothing.

JOEY. He's the one that's never mentioned me.

SAM. You never mentioned him either.

JOEY. Oh, I'm sorry – when was I meant to do that? Before or after you rammed your tongue down my throat?

SAM. You licked me.

JOEY. You kissed me.

SAM. I didn't know you were George's daughter.

JOEY. You only kiss strangers?

SAM. No. I don't really kiss people, at all, usually; just you.

JOEY. Oh.

Beat.

SAM. Can I do it again?

JOEY. What?

SAM. Kiss you.

JOEY. They're right about you Americans being greedy, aren't they?

SAM. You're pretty funny; and pretty… and funny.

JOEY. Sam – I –

SAM (*interrupting*). Can I kiss you?

JOEY. Don't ask that, no one asks that, well, Americans probably ask but we don't –

SAM *lunges forward to kiss* JOEY.

JOEY *lurches out of the way.*

I didn't mean do it!

SAM. You said 'don't ask'!

JOEY. I meant 'don't ask' as in read between the bloody lines. My body was not saying 'come hither'.

SAM. Why not?

JOEY. What?

SAM. Why wasn't your body saying 'come hither'?

JOEY. I don't know.

SAM. Last night you put your hand in my back pocket, then you licked my face and dragged me through New York. In American, that means 'come hither'.

Beat.

JOEY. I was very tired.

SAM. Tired?

JOEY. Yes.

SAM. Sure.

JOEY. Look, Sam, I'm sure you're really nice, you seem really nice.

SAM. I am.

JOEY. Okay.

SAM. You seem – amazing.

JOEY. That wasn't quite where I was –

SAM. I think you're a bit amazing. I know it's crazy 'cos I just met you but I think, I think you're kind of amazing.

JOEY. Okay, Sam – why don't we play a game where you say the exact opposite of what you're thinking. I think it might help with the language barrier.

SAM. No.

JOEY. Why not?

SAM. I'd started.

JOEY. Oh right, I see.

SAM. The idea of doing you makes me sick.

JOEY. Good.

SAM. I've never thought about what you look like naked.

JOEY. That's a little easy to decipher.

SAM. English girls are real warm and friendly.

JOEY *gives a sardonic smile.*

Why don't you want me to tell you that I like you?

JOEY. Wait, I can't work out the opposite of –

SAM (*interrupting*). I stopped playing.

JOEY. Yes, I know, I was… I don't know why I don't like it; it makes me feel uncomfortable.

SAM. Why?

JOEY. I don't know.

SAM. It's a shame; I could do it all day.

They look at one another.

Beat.

JOEY. The more you say it the less I believe it.

SAM. That makes no sense.

JOEY. Does to me.

SAM. Guess I'd better shut up.

JOEY *smiles.*

SAM *exits.*

Two

The sitting room.

It's one o'clock.

GEORGE *enters, he's out of breath.*

GEORGE *is carrying a bunch of white roses.*

GEORGE *starts trying to arrange the roses.*

JOEY *enters.*

JOEY. Hello.

GEORGE. Were you sleeping?

JOEY. No.

GEORGE. It's a lovely day out, bright sunshine, you should have a roam.

JOEY. It's freezing out there. You want a hand with those?

GEORGE. Not at all.

JOEY. They're my favourites.

GEORGE. God knows where you have to go to grow a rose in bloody December but nevertheless; they look rather good, don't they?

JOEY. Perfect.

Pause.

GEORGE. Why don't you go and help Sam with lunch?

JOEY. No, I'm okay here. I'm reading.

Beat.

GEORGE. That yours?

JOEY. What?

GEORGE. The paper?

JOEY. Oh yeah, I got it yesterday, for the flight.

GEORGE. I see university has had its way with you.

JOEY. What?

GEORGE. *Guardian.*

JOEY. Sure.

GEORGE. How is it?

JOEY. The paper?

GEORGE. University.

JOEY. I graduated. You sent me a congratulations card.

GEORGE (*works hard*). You said you were going to do a Masters in Politics and Religion, focusing on the contemporary relationship between Church and State.

Beat.

JOEY. I didn't get funding.

GEORGE. Why not?

JOEY. Because there isn't any.

GEORGE. Couldn't your mother –

JOEY. Mum didn't have the cash.

GEORGE. And –

JOEY (*interrupting*). I'm not his responsibility. Careful, you'll spill the water.

GEORGE. Surely he could have seen his way to –

JOEY (*interrupting*). I wouldn't have taken it even if he'd offered.

Beat.

GEORGE. You should have rung.

JOEY. I did.

GEORGE. What are you doing for money?

JOEY. I worked in a bar.

GEORGE. Worked?

JOEY. Yes.

GEORGE. What happened?

JOEY. Overstaffed.

GEORGE. From what I remember of the last time the economy nosedived; it didn't stop people from drinking.

JOEY. Overstaffed, Dad. Too many staff; management can't afford to pay their staff.

GEORGE. It's Christmas.

JOEY. Too big to be an elf it turns out; fucking shame because I do suit green.

GEORGE. I don't like your tone.

JOEY. Of course you don't.

Pause.

GEORGE. You could have been unpleasant by phone.

JOEY. I don't want to be unpleasant, I want – can we turn up the carols?

GEORGE. Of course.

JOEY turns up the carols.

JOEY. You should get a tree.

GEORGE. Little late in the day. Have you rung your mother?

JOEY. No.

GEORGE. You should ring her.

JOEY. Why?

GEORGE. It's good manners to let people know where you are.

JOEY. Really. You didn't.

GEORGE knocks over the vase, the water spills all over the table.

GEORGE. Fuck!

JOEY. Language.

GEORGE. Can you get a cloth?

JOEY exits.

GEORGE tries to stop his hand from shaking.

JOEY *re-enters*.

GEORGE *asks for the cloth*.

JOEY. I'll do it, sit down.

GEORGE. No –

JOEY (*interrupting*). I'll do it.

Some time passes. JOEY *cleans in silence*.

GEORGE. How is she?

JOEY. Fine (*Beat*.) They've had another baby, girl, Ahdia-Jessica, cute as hell.

GEORGE. I'm sure.

JOEY. The house is covered in toys.

GEORGE. Bet she doesn't like that.

JOEY. There weren't any decorations. No Christmas tree, no wreath, no presents.

GEORGE. Give me that cloth; you've missed half of it.

Some time passes.

JOEY. It's different. It smells different. They've painted the kitchen orange. They've made my old bedroom into a nursery.

GEORGE. Where does he put his books?

JOEY. He reads them on his computer.

GEORGE. As if there was any further proof needed of that man's –

JOEY. The books aren't the point, Dad.

GEORGE. Would you like a drink?

JOEY. No.

Pause.

GEORGE. Those roses look rather lovely.

JOEY. Mum's started wearing a headscarf, which is fine, it's just, she's my mum so... Dad?

GEORGE. Yes?

Pause.

It must be nearly lunch, my stomach's rumbling.

JOEY. Dad – can I stay, a while?

GEORGE. Sam's bound to be incinerating dinner I'm going to go and –

JOEY. Dad?

GEORGE. Sam!

JOEY. Who the hell is he anyway?

GEORGE. What?

JOEY. It's a bit weird, isn't it? Playing house with a teenager?

GEORGE. Playing house?

JOEY. Well?

GEORGE. He's – he – he helps me around the place, sometimes – he's – he's here because I pay him to be here.

JOEY. You pay him? To clean?

GEORGE. Yes.

JOEY. And to spend Christmases with you?

GEORGE. Please stop manipulating the situation, he helps me – that's all.

JOEY. But I don't get it – helps you do what?

GEORGE. Things your mother used to do!

Beat.

JOEY. I can teach you how to iron a shirt.

GEORGE. Boil an egg?

JOEY. Poach them even.

GEORGE. Oh, I don't want to rush things.

Pause.

JOEY. Dad – please, can I stay just for a –

GEORGE (*interrupting*). Joanna, I haven't seen you for two years.

JOEY. That's hardly my fault.

GEORGE. You should have rung or written or –

JOEY. It's not like you're busy!

GEORGE. You can't just turn up here at four in the bloody morning with no explanation –

JOEY. I'm trying to explain.

GEORGE. Soaked to the skin, make-up all over your face and stinking to high heaven of booze!

JOEY. I didn't *stink* of –

GEORGE (*interrupting*). And this morning I discover that you've spent half the night enjoying all manner of high-jinks with my employee – I'm still braced for the arrival of the police, or the angry lover, or the wail of an abandoned infant from the dumpster.

JOEY. Dustbin.

GEORGE. Dustbin.

Beat.

JOEY. Well, thank you for your welcome.

GEORGE. Thank you for your w-warning.

GEORGE exits.

JOEY is left standing.

Three

SAM *and* JOEY *are surrounded by boxes.*

SAM *rips off a large piece of tape – it makes a loud noise.*

JOEY. Fuck's sake, Sam, shh! You'll wake him up!

SAM. Sorry!

JOEY. What does it look like?

SAM. I can't open it without making any noise.

JOEY. Do it quietly.

SAM. It's tape!

JOEY. We can put it in the corner – we can make paper chains.

SAM. Popcorn strings.

JOEY. Paper chains.

SAM. Okay.

JOEY. And we'll put the nativity on the table and we'll put a star on the top of the tree and cinnamon sticks and decorations and we'll play carols and if we have time we can make mulled wine and it'll all smell amazing – oooh – it's exciting. He's going to like it, right?

SAM. You sure he's the kind of guy that goes in for surprises?

JOEY. You think he won't like it?

Beat.

SAM. He'll love it. Course he will, he'll fucking love it. Okay – so action plan, tree first?

JOEY. Yes. I'll go and get the scissors, you put some carols on!

SAM. Aye aye, captain.

JOEY *exits*.

SAM *impatiently pulls the tree out of the box*.

The tree is bright neon pink.

JOEY *enters*.

JOEY. Oh. You didn't need the scissors.

SAM. Nope.

JOEY. It's meant to be green.

SAM. The one in the shop was green. We could spray it?

JOEY. We don't have any spray.

SAM. We've totally got enough stuff to cover it.

JOEY. There aren't enough paper chains in the entire world to stop that tree being pink, Sam.

SAM. I guess. I'm sorry – I should have checked the box, but look, it's totally not the end of the world we can still do all the other stuff, there's the nativity and the mistletoe and the candles and the wine – it'll be amazing, it'll just be treeless. Who cares about trees anyway? Totally overrated.

JOEY. Yeah, I guess.

SAM. You do the nativity and I'll do the mistletoe; give me the scissors, the nativity is in the newspaper wrap in the blue bag – get it out, we'll set it up on the table.

JOEY. Why are you helping me?

SAM. What?

JOEY. I've been really unpleasant to you ever since I got here and you're still helping me.

SAM. Sure.

JOEY. Why?

SAM. I want to.

JOEY. I just don't want you to... you're not going to get in my pants.

SAM. Your pants?

JOEY. I'm not going to sleep with you.

SAM. Oh, I know, I'm not... I'm helping you because I want to.

JOEY. Right.

SAM. 'Cos you kind of seem like you could do with some help. (*Beat.*) Come on, unwrap – we're against the clock here.

JOEY. Okay, okay.

JOEY *starts unwrapping the nativity.*

SAM. Can you pass me the string, it's on the top there?

JOEY. Sure.

SAM. Oh look, we're both under the –

JOEY. Are you done with the string?

SAM *throws the string at* JOEY.

JOEY *goes to put the string back on the side and spots the blister pack.*

What's this?

SAM. Hm?

JOEY. It's a pill-box thing.

SAM. Oh, I don't know, I can't see it. I thought you were doing the –

JOEY (*interrupting*). It's full of pills, are they Dad's?

SAM. No.

JOEY. Whose are they?

SAM. Mine.

JOEY. What for? Sorry, is that rude, I didn't mean to –

SAM (*interrupting*). ADHD.

JOEY. Oh. Right; gosh – that kind of makes more sense of –

SAM. Thanks.

JOEY. Sorry, I didn't mean to be rude.

SAM. Oh no, don't sweat it. Mistletoe – check. Wine – I'll go and put the wine on, that nativity better be done by the time I get back –

SAM *goes to exit and pockets the medication.*

JOEY. Where did you get the nativity?

SAM. Same place I got the tree, it was the only place open. You know where we put the oranges for the wine?

JOEY. Mary's purple.

SAM. No fucking way, that's cool, man.

JOEY. She's purple and glittery.

SAM. That's not right, right?

JOEY. There's a giraffe.

SAM. That's totally a camel.

JOEY. It's a giraffe. It's in the same bundle as a rhino.

SAM. You don't think that's cool, do you?

JOEY. No.

SAM. I'm sorry – I just, he just said it was all there, so I...

JOEY. None of it looks right. This was –

SAM (*interrupting*). No, come on, come on, you just got to –

JOEY. It's all cheap and new and shit and –

SAM. It's good, you just got to set it up right and get the lighting right and –

JOEY. There's a fucking pink tree and a giraffe and fake fucking snow, none of it feels or looks like Christmas.

SAM. It's okay, we just got to –

JOEY. Stop saying 'it's okay' when it's not, Sam, it makes you sound like a fucking idiot!

Beat.

SAM. You'll wake George up.

JOEY. He's not a baby.

SAM. I thought you wanted it to be a surprise.

JOEY. It looks like he's been burgled by Elton fucking John. Let's pack it away – let's just throw it all away.

SAM. What do you want it to look like?

JOEY. It's meant to look – look – older.

SAM. We could just wait a while.

JOEY. You ever have those memories where you can't work out if they ever actually happened or you've just looked at the photograph so many times that you think they did?

SAM. Sure – Jenna Jameson.

JOEY. Why can't you be sad?

SAM. It's Christmas, who wants to be sad?

JOEY. We should tidy this shit up before Dad comes in.

SAM. What did it smell like?

JOEY. What?

SAM. Well, photographs don't smell of anything so if the memory smells like something then it's got to be real.

JOEY. Cinnamon, cinnamon and oranges.

SAM. Come here.

JOEY. What?

SAM. Come here.

SAM *collects a crap candle that's in one of the bags.*

SAM *lights the candle and gives* JOEY *the orange.*

JOEY. What are you doing?

SAM. Close your eyes, stick your nail in this.

SAM *gives* JOEY *an orange.*

SAM *lights the candle.*

Sniff.

JOEY *smiles.*

And we can even get a little fake snow and –

JOEY. Sam – that's aerosol.

SAM. Oh.

JOEY. You'll blow my face off.

SAM. Okay, well – we'll get our glittery Mary and we'll turn her upside down, you don't mind do you, Mary? No you don't. She's real tolerant see? She doesn't bitch all the time and we'll just sprinkle her magic dust all over the place and you look real close and it smells like Christmas and it's pretty much snowing.

SAM *shakes the Mary and glitter falls off it.*

JOEY *sits, eyes closed, nose above a candle, holding an orange and getting covered in purple sparkly stuff from the crap Mary.*

The glitter falls over the flame.

There is something a little wondrous about it.

Time passes.

Eventually the pair start to tidy.

It seems there is a little peace.

Meanwhile, GEORGE *enters the bathroom.*

In the sitting room, JOEY *blows out the candle.* SAM *and* JOEY *exit.*

GEORGE *is trying to shave.*

This should take a few minutes.

The effort is extraordinary.

His hand shakes badly.

The attempt is unsuccessful.

As frustration culminates, GEORGE *slams the sink, careful not to be overheard.*

GEORGE *wipes his face.*

SAM *and* JOEY *enter the sitting room.*

SAM *is still holding mistletoe.*

JOEY. It's never going to happen.

SAM. I just like the look of it.

GEORGE *enters.*

JOEY. Dad?

GEORGE. It smells of cinnamon.

JOEY. Yes.

GEORGE. That's nice.

SAM. How d'you sleep?

GEORGE. Well, thank you. That meal could've sedated a rhino, mind.

SAM. Thanks.

JOEY. I thought we might play Trivial Pursuit?

GEORGE. God, where did you find that?

JOEY. In the cupboard.

GEORGE. I'm not sure I'm in the mood.

JOEY. Dad, come on – indulge me.

GEORGE. I'm tired.

JOEY. You just had a nap.

GEORGE. Sam, why don't you play?

JOEY. Where's the harm? We play for half an hour, you win by a staggeringly huge lead, I moan about my tiddler of a brain – and the world's natural balance is redressed – perfect.

SAM. Come on, Joey, I can play.

JOEY. I want you to play, Dad.

GEORGE. You sound like a four-year-old.

SAM. Why don't I get some drinks? Wine? Bucks stuff?

JOEY. Wine would be great.

GEORGE. Could you get me a whisky mac?

SAM. Sure. Joey – wine?

JOEY. Thanks – more –

SAM. You sure?

JOEY. Yes. Thank you.

    Pause.

GEORGE. That cinnamon really does –

JOEY. Please, Dad, just one game.

SAM. Joey – I don't think –

GEORGE (*interrupting*). One round – no more.

JOEY. Yess.

SAM. George, if you don't want to – I can do it.

JOEY. Shut up.

SAM. He shouldn't have to just because –

JOEY (*interrupting*). You're such a two-faced –

GEORGE (*interrupting*). It's fine, come on, let's give the little
madam what she wants.

JOEY. Oh, don't be like that otherwise there's no point.

GEORGE. Come on, set it up. Pass me the cards, I'll shuffle
them.

GEORGE *begins to read them.*

JOEY. Shuffle, not read, Dad – no cheating.

GEORGE. Alright.

JOEY. Sam, hurry up – we're ready.

SAM. Okay, good, okay. Let's get involved here – I warn you
though, I'm crazy competitive.

JOEY. I'm terrified. Okay, Dad, first question –

SAM. Elvis!

JOEY. No way! How did you know?

SAM. Seriously?

JOEY. No, you twat.

SAM. Whoa.

GEORGE. He was being funny. Let's start again –

JOEY. Right, Dad, without interruption – first question, 'What
is the title of J. D. Salinger's most famous novel?'

GEORGE. *Catcher in the Rye.*

JOEY. Yup. Sam, roll. Okay. You won't get this –

SAM. I might.

JOEY. You won't – 'How many muscles are there in your
hand?'

SAM. Um,

JOEY. Tick, tick, tick –

SAM. I don't know, like one in each finger –

JOEY. I knew it –

SAM. – none, they're all tendons.

JOEY. What? How did you know that?

SAM. Full of surprises. Right, I'll ask – roll.

JOEY. I don't trust him to ask.

GEORGE. For God's sake.

JOEY. Fine, ask – but I never pretended I was any good at this.

SAM. Okay, right – okay – 'Mick Jagger was lead singer of which –'

JOEY. Rolling Stones.

SAM. The difficulty level of these questions is pretty varied, isn't it?

JOEY. Dad, your go – roll.

GEORGE. Right, four, Arts and Literature.

SAM. Anyone for anything to eat or…?

JOEY. We're playing.

SAM. I just thought… George, you okay for –

GEORGE (*interrupting*). I'm fine, Sam. Joey – ask the question.

JOEY. 'In linguistics, what is the name of the smallest structural unit of meaning?'

GEORGE *searches*.

SAM. You lost me –

JOEY. No shit. Come on, Dad, enlighten the boy.

GEORGE. This whisky's gone straight to my head.

JOEY. Dad, hurry up – come on.

GEORGE. It's right there – it's – it's –

JOEY. Dad?

SAM. Give him a second.

JOEY. Will you just shut up?

GEORGE. Come on, of course, I'm joking – it's too easy for
me, it's my field, ask me another – something about the
Spice Girls or the – the –

JOEY. No, go on – just answer it, it's fine.

SAM. No, give him another – it's too easy –

JOEY. Dad – answer.

SAM. Just give me the box, I'll take another –

JOEY. No, Dad, just say the answer, take the point.

SAM. Give me the box.

JOEY. Dad!

    SAM *snatches another card.*

SAM. George, 'By what name do Canadians refer to the Union
Jack?'

JOEY. No way, he can answer the other one.

GEORGE. Please, can we stop a minute?

JOEY. Dad, answer the original one.

    SAM *mouths the answer to* GEORGE.

    JOEY *catches them cheating.*

    Why the fuck are you cheating?

SAM. Joey –

JOEY. Why?

GEORGE. I'm going to bed.

JOEY. You've only just got up.

GEORGE. And I'm still tired.

JOEY. It's Christmas Day.

GEORGE. Joanna, stop being so childish.

JOEY. A child? I'm barely a fucking guest!

GEORGE. Get out!

> JOEY *grabs* SAM*'s coat off the back of the door and exits.*
>
> *Silence… some time passes.*
>
> GEORGE *turns and heads towards his bedroom.*

SAM. I'm sorry.

GEORGE. It's not your fault.

SAM. She knows something's not right, George, she's a smart girl.

> *Pause.*

I think she needs her dad.

GEORGE. I know that.

> GEORGE *exits.*

Four

The sitting room.

The lights are off.

SAM *is watching television.*

It's ten o'clock at night.

JOEY *enters.*

SAM. Hey.

JOEY. You're still here?

SAM. I couldn't leave.

JOEY. That's kind of you.

SAM. You took my coat.

JOEY. Oh.

    JOEY *takes off* SAM*'s coat.*

SAM. Where have you been?

JOEY. Is he –

SAM (*interrupting*). He stayed up for ages, he was worried, he
    asked me to stick about, to wait, he –

JOEY (*interrupting*). Yeah. I bet.

    Beat.

SAM. He didn't mean –

JOEY (*interrupting*). Sam, you shouldn't have to tell me that.

    Beat.

SAM. You must be freezing.

JOEY. Why were you cheating?

SAM. Where you been?

JOEY. Why were you giving him the answers, Sam? Listen to
    me, why? He's the smartest man I know, he was a professor
    for twenty years – you know that?

SAM. Yeah.

JOEY. Oh, he told you that? Of course he did. Well, he can win
    Trivial Pursuit in his sleep, so why the fuck were you
    cheating?

    Beat.

SAM. I wanted to help him.

JOEY. Because that's all you want to do, isn't it? You just want to help; you just want to help everyone!

SAM. What's wrong with that?

JOEY. He didn't need your help.

SAM. I'm sorry.

JOEY. I don't need your help!

SAM. No.

JOEY. So, what are you doing still doing here, Sam?

SAM. He asked me to stay to check you were in safe and you are so I'm done, I'll go – I'm going.

JOEY. You know what, Sam? I think it's a bit fucked up a nineteen-year-old boy spending all his time with a sixty-year-old man.

SAM. Yeah?

JOEY. Watching all your old movies, shuffling around making Dad his bucks fizz and his tea just the way he likes it, letting him shout at you and order you about and... do you like it, secretly? Knowing someone's boss, all wise and knowing; feeling like someone has all the answers? 'Yes sir, no sir!'

SAM. Is this making you feel better?

JOEY. Yes.

SAM. Fine. Go ahead.

JOEY. Oh, don't go and take all the fun out of it.

SAM. Cutting me down is not going to make you feel any taller.

JOEY. Listen to yourself; you're a walking fucking fortune cookie!

SAM. You're not angry with me.

JOEY. Aren't I? Aren't I? Because I can't shake the feeling, Sam, that you, you and all your smiling and your starry-eyed fucking – I just walked up Fifth Avenue – and it's all big and shiny and the cars are huge and the buildings all stretching themselves up into the stars and lights on Broadway all shouting their success into the night like everyone is just bound to be a big success! And then you go and sit in a café and all the waitresses are failed actresses and failed singers and on the subway there are a billion adverts for pissy little classes and you just know those waitresses are going to be serving coffee for the rest of their fucking lives!

SAM. What's wrong with being a waitress?

JOEY. I just can't help but feel, Sam – all that dreaming – it suddenly feels like the most stupid fucking idea you ever had and all those stars and buildings, all those chandeliers and even the kisses; it all feels like lies.

Beat.

SAM. When I moved here, I was sixteen. I was so scared; I didn't think I was going to get anywhere. I knew I wanted to be a doctor so badly but I didn't have the money or the grades or… and I was staying in this shitty shitty little apartment and it was fucking freezing and I used to go to bed every night and I'd just repeat and repeat to myself, 'if you're going to make your way in the world, it's going to take everything you got.'

JOEY. Sam?

SAM. Yeah.

JOEY. You know what that is?

SAM. What?

JOEY. That is the theme tune from *Cheers*.

SAM. Who cares? Who fucking cares? Sometimes a fucking bumper sticker can save someone's life.

JOEY. But it's not real, none of it's real!

SAM. You can't believe in anything, can you?

JOEY. Come on then, Sam, enlighten me, what is it that you believe in, hm?

SAM. God, my country, my family…

JOEY. Where I come from you're a nutter if you think those things even exist.

SAM. Myself.

Beat.

JOEY. I – I've spent my whole life jumping through these hoops that were meant to lead somewhere, I worked my arse off at school, at each stage, GCSEs, A-levels, I busted a fucking gut at uni whilst everyone else was getting pissed and getting laid and it was all meant to be so that when I left, I'd – I'd land somewhere. But it's like I made through the final hoop, fucking degree in my hand and smile on my face, ready to enjoy my job and my security and then someone just smacked me in the face with a fucking spade. I got sacked from a bar job, there aren't any other crap jobs left, I haven't landed anywhere.

SAM. So go home.

JOEY. I don't know where to go.

SAM. What about your mum?

JOEY. They eat food that I don't know how to cook and say prayers before eating that I don't understand, my mum – my mum wears clothes that I don't know where to buy them. My bedroom is now the bedroom of a little girl –

SAM (*interrupting*). Your sister.

JOEY. – who speaks a different language to me.

SAM. So learn.

JOEY. I'm scared. I'm scared I'll disappear.

Pause.

SAM. You got to know where you come from if you want to know where you're going.

JOEY *laughs*.

What?

JOEY. How do you not feel awkward saying that shit?

SAM. I'm not wrong.

JOEY. No.

SAM. Well then.

JOEY. How do you know?

SAM. Where I come from? I'm an American, it's easy, we got it written down.

JOEY. Sometimes I'm jealous of – of – people that are fighting wars.

SAM. What?

JOEY. I watch history programmes about the Second World War or the Civil Rights Movement or I watch the news and see people screaming and shouting and I sometimes want to be among it, sometimes I touch the TV screen and wish myself into the middle of it all. Does that make you angry?

SAM. No.

JOEY. I want to stand in a group and say 'we are this. We know we are this. We can *see* that we are this; we will fight to be this.'

SAM. White people have been doing that for hundreds and hundreds –

JOEY. But I want to be on the other side, I want to be on the right side. I want to be good. I want to be part of good people. I want to be proud.

SAM. You got to be proud of where you come from.

JOEY. But I don't know what it is; I don't know what we, I don't know what I look like.

Pause.

SAM. Dance with me?

JOEY. What?

SAM. Dance with me?

JOEY. How – how do you say the things you do and believe them, like, how do you keep a straight face?

SAM. What have I got to lose?

JOEY. Pride.

SAM. Will you dance with me?

JOEY. No.

SAM. Dance with me.

JOEY. There's no music.

SAM *switches on the radio.*

'Fairytale of New York' by The Pogues plays.

SAM. Now there is. Dance with me.

JOEY. To this? You must be fucking kidding.

SAM *takes* JOEY*'s hand.*

SAM. Shut up.

The music kicks off.

JOEY *dances.*

JOEY *is wild with it.*

They dance, they jig, they stomp and spin with wild abandon.

Youth in all its optimistic fury flails bumps and grinds across the stage.

GEORGE *enters.*

GEORGE *has a large gash from shaving down his face.*

GEORGE *is dripping blood.*

GEORGE *doesn't know where he is.*

JOEY. Dad?

SAM. Turn the music off.

JOEY. Dad?

SAM. I've got it, don't worry – turn the music off!

JOEY *goes to turn the music off.*

George, what are you doing, buddy?

GEORGE. I don't... I don't...

GEORGE *is on the verge of tears.*

SAM. Come on, buddy. Come on.

SAM *and* GEORGE *exit.*

JOEY *stands.*

End of Act Two.

ACT THREE

One

GEORGE (*to audience*). A man, I have always felt, has his
mind, whereas a woman has her heart; a fact that has caused
much heartache and many headaches through the years.
When disaster strikes, a gentleman, such as myself, runs to
his cool and calm and satisfying arsenal of rationale, indeed
my mind was my occupation, my brain my bread and butter,
after all. And now – there – like a sh, sh – shadow – the connection. And I am lost. And I am lost.

She left me for a Muslim man, this I understood – stand. He
knew who he was, you see, he had history – his culture was
potent, he was validated, located, connected, reinforced. I was
somewhat awash, at sea – wishy-washy – and I learnt that this
can be a little unnerving for a mother, a wife, my lover.

My wife had been my greatest achievement. There comes a
time, the elder gentlemen will concur, when, when one faces
– *struggling* – the reckoning. When one weighs – his wife,
his cars, his houses, his wage – you weigh your present
against the dreams you had as a child and woe betide the
man that falls short. For to arrive at a destination that doesn't
satisfy – well, there is little room left now for improvement.

What I have is what I have – well, not exactly. What I have –
is what I had. It is less and less every day and I was not
satisfied with what I had when I started. So you see it is a
bleak and terminal affair, if I let it cross my mind. Mind. At
times I don't mind.

And then there is her. I can suffer the panic of a dark night,
the claustrophobia of an irreparable situation – I can suffer
that, but were she to get even a glimpse of this; a glimpse –
if she should see her father as a fool, that, I don't think I

could bear. She should leave – take with her her precious, talented youth and hide it from me. I sleep with tens of photographs of her, surrounding me, so I can try to keep her in my head. But – I am aware, I – one day I will have the in-in-indecency to forget her, to misplace her and no child should have to suffer that. She should leave, leave me before she realises I will be leaving her.

JOEY *enters*.

JOEY. Dad?

GEORGE. Yes.

JOEY. What are you doing sitting in the dark?

GEORGE. I'm sorry if I startled you.

JOEY. Would you like a cup of tea?

GEORGE. No, no.

JOEY. Are you okay?

GEORGE. Yes.

JOEY. Whisky?

GEORGE. I'm fine.

Pause.

JOEY. Dad – what's –

GEORGE. Just a scratch. I cut myself with the bloody razor.

JOEY. No I –

GEORGE. Why don't you pop that lamp on?

JOEY *turns the lamp on*.

JOEY. I got you a present.

GEORGE. Oh, you shouldn't do that you –

JOEY. Don't worry, didn't break the bank.

JOEY *gives* GEORGE *the present*.

It's a bit egotistical really.

GEORGE *unwraps the present – a photograph of* JOEY.

Thought you could put it up, around somewhere. Just so I'm saying 'hey', even if I'm not here.

GEORGE. Thank you. It's lovely. (*Beat.*) Look in the sideboard, there, there's a box.

JOEY *finds the parcel.*

I was going to send it – I...

JOEY *unwraps the present, she holds the earrings up.*

JOEY. They're lovely.

GEORGE. I was going to get a book, like normal – I just thought – something that sparkles, why not?

JOEY. Why not.

They smile.

Why won't you tell me?

Beat.

GEORGE. Give us a hug.

JOEY *hugs* GEORGE.

Sorry for being such a beast, JoJo.

JOEY. You smell like Dad. Well done.

GEORGE. Oh, thank you, gold star.

JOEY. Yes; definitely.

Beat.

I think Sam and me –

GEORGE. I –

JOEY. I think Sam and I are going to sit on the roof for a bit before bed, look at the lights. Would you like to come?

GEORGE. No, you're alright. Have fun.

JOEY. Will do.

GEORGE. Tell Sam it's about bloody time he went home.

JOEY. Oh, I think he was going to stay tonight.

GEORGE. What?

JOEY. It was a joke.

GEORGE. Right. Well –

Beat.

It would of course be fine if that was the case.

JOEY. Sleep well, Dads.

GEORGE. Nighto.

JOEY exits.

Two

JOEY and SAM sit on the roof and look out across New York City.

JOEY. Don't you think it looks like a massive crossword.

SAM. Crossword? How?

JOEY. Look, all the windows with their lights on are like the empty squares ready to put the letters in and all the windows with lights that are off look like the black squares in between.

SAM. I don't see it. I always think it looks a bit like toothpicks.

JOEY. Toothpicks? What the fuck kind of toothpicks do you use?

Beat.

What's wrong with him, Sam?

SAM. He's ill.

JOEY. I'd got that far.

SAM. He – he –

JOEY. Please.

SAM. He doesn't want you to know.

JOEY. He's my dad, Sam.

SAM. He has early onset Lewy body dementia.

JOEY. Dementia?

SAM. Yeah.

Beat.

JOEY. What does that, um, does that –

SAM. It comes in bursts, sometimes he's fine and other times he hears things or sees things or forgets things; he gets confused, he has trouble with movement, he –

JOEY. No, I mean, um – is he… is he going to get better?

SAM. No.

JOEY. Right.

Pause.

How long?

SAM. You can't really tell.

JOEY. Roughly, give or take –

SAM. Life expectancy following diagnosis is between five and seven years.

JOEY. And when we was he, um – ?

SAM. Just over –

JOEY (*interrupting*). Two years.

SAM. Yeah.

JOEY. I thought he was embarrassed, by Mum and work and – I thought he was a coward.

SAM. He doesn't want people to know.

JOEY. He's just going to sit over here, miles away from anyone, and disappear?

SAM. I don't know, I –

JOEY. I need him. I – Sam, I don't want him to forget me.

Three

JOEY (*to audience*). It's a movement, isn't it? That's what they call it. When people feel the same thing in their soul at the same time – they call it a movement. I've always been jealous that I never got to ban the bomb, or burn my bras, jealous of people that lived through the war because, well, they had a common enemy and that'd make you want to fight and it'd make it clear what you were fighting for and it might even allow for a hero or two.

I said this to Sam, who, it transpired, one got used to over time – sure there were differences; sex, for example. I liked the British kind, angsty, passionate but essentially joyless and for him, well it was sort of like going to the Oscars, lots of tears and thank-yous and I felt he struggled with an overwhelming urge to clap at the end.

We sat with Dad, and played board games and talked and – Sam would take over when Dad forgot things, or when I found dirty plates in the cupboard or his shaving stuff in the cutlery drawer, or once when he struggled for my name – Sam stepped in at times when I just couldn't really stop myself from finding it all horribly sad. (*Controls tears.*)

In January Sam took me away for the weekend – and when we got to Washington, strangers were high-fiving each other and smiling and everyone seemed so – excited. It was that same feeling I'd had, on that rooftop on Christmas Day, right in the pit of my stomach, looking at all those tiny lights holding tiny lives and knowing that they were part of something – but that something was bigger than them – and it was good. And when it came to it, with the sun peeking itself out behind the Washington Monument, and looking down The Mall and seeing two million people waiting, exercising the muscle of – faith – well, I thought that it didn't really matter what you believed in – just as long as you knew how to believe.

And just as he appeared and all the flags started waving and young kids started whooping and older men and women shed some quieter tears, Sam turned to me and he wrapped me right up in his scarf and he said –

'Now, you've got to believe in this – right?'

And I looked at him, and he had this stupid smile on his face, grinning ear to fucking ear, and suddenly I realised what kind of balls it takes just to think that the world isn't such a bad place.

But of course, Sam, Dad, even that new President of theirs, they weren't really mine to believe in, not for ever anyway. No, us British, English – well, me – I'm not like them, I'm not flying the flag of revolution, I don't have fire in my belly or idealism on my tongue and I'm not singing the song of change and why? Because I don't know the words yet; but I will, we will. I won't be forgotten.

Barack Obama's inaugural speech is heard.

VOICEOVER. 'It's the answer that led those who have been told for so long by so many to be cynical, and fearful, and doubtful of what we can achieve to put their hands on the arc of history and bend it once more toward the hope of a better day. It's been a long time coming, but tonight, because of what we did on this day, in this election, at this defining moment, change has come to America.'

EPILOGUE

SAM (*to audience*). It's the spring of 2011 and the night is clear and promising and it feels like it's the first time it's ever been that way. I'm twenty-one and in front of me, London Town; the sun is real low in the sky, the clouds are pink and the birds are black and the river's running gold.

Evening-dinner people are drinking beers and eating burgers, rube boys on BMXs, swanky-looking people, skanky-looking people – and right in the middle of it, sliding between the clowns and the couples and the conversations – walking right this way, almost here, almost close enough to touch, not knowing I'm looking right at her...

Hey.

JOEY. Hey.

Beat.

You look different.

SAM. Do I?

JOEY. Older, I guess.

JOEY *kisses* SAM *on the cheek.*

SAM (*to audience*). She smells the same.

JOEY. Have you had a tiny stroke?

SAM. No.

(*To audience.*) We sit – riverside. The lights in the trees look like luminous fruit; she bends her head back and looks up – I want to run my tongue along the line of her neck.

JOEY. It's hot, eh?

SAM. It's hotter at home; sweaty as hell.

JOEY. I can't imagine it not being cold.

SAM. How are you?

> (*To audience.*) She doesn't look at me. She watches a bird picking over an ice-cream cone. She has three freckles on the left side of her nose, I remember being in bed and putting my fingers on them as if her head was a bowling ball.

JOEY. Tired, but okay. You?

SAM. Good, it's good to see you. I got – these are –

> SAM *gives* JOEY *a small bunch of white roses.*

JOEY. Thanks.

SAM. They're from the – they covered the whole place in them. Hundreds and hundreds all over the –

JOEY (*interrupting*). Sure.

SAM. I'm sorry if getting your number was –

JOEY. It's fine.

SAM (*to audience*). She looks me straight in the face for the first time.

JOEY. I should have – I meant to, but I – I just in the end, I –

SAM. It's fine.

JOEY. It's not really. I bet people thought –

SAM (*interrupting*). Who cares?

JOEY. Was my mum –

SAM (*interrupting*). I spotted her immediately. You look just like her. She's beautiful.

> JOEY *laughs.*

> (*To audience.*) Bang, right there. Teeth and eyes; it's so good it makes my stomach hurt.

SAM. What?

JOEY. I forgot how easily you –

SAM. Maybe I'm just used to beautiful women.

JOEY. Maybe. (*Beat.*) Was she –

SAM. She was alone.

JOEY. She gave you my number?

SAM. I asked. I – I really wanted to see you.

> (*To audience.*) I want to cook my mum's bolognese for her, tomorrow evening I'll cook my mum's bolognese for her.

JOEY. I have to get back to work, Sam.

SAM. What time do you finish?

JOEY. I've two jobs I go to –

SAM. Where you working?

JOEY. That place, there – with the white awning.

SAM. You're serving coffee?

JOEY. In the daytime.

SAM. And in the night-time you're –

JOEY. I work for a travel magazine, for free – just experience – I'm an expert on Puerto Rico.

SAM. You get to travel, that's great, that's amazing –

> (*To audience.*) My head is full of five hundred Puerto Rican men and flight-transfer timetables – Puerto Rico to JFK.

JOEY. No, I get to Google.

SAM. Oh.

> (*To audience.*) Heathrow – JFK.

JOEY. Sam – I really have to –

SAM. I have some things for you – he wanted me to give you some –

JOEY (*interrupting*). I don't want them.

SAM. Joey?

JOEY. You started med school yet or –?

SAM. Oh – almost, yeah, real close – just I broke my leg
    beginning of the year and –

JOEY. Jumping down fire escapes?

SAM. Sure, something like that. It kinda blew my savings so – I
    need to work just a little longer just to –

JOEY. Shouldn't be buying plane tickets to England.

SAM. I wanted to, it seemed like a good way to –

JOEY. You staying around long?

SAM. I don't know.

JOEY. Few days or –?

SAM. Yeah, I guess, I'll take a look about.

JOEY. Where are you staying?

SAM (*to audience*). I want to wake up with her hair wrapped
    round my thumb.

    North.

JOEY. Really? Whereabouts? I live in the north.

SAM. It might be west, some hostel, place.

JOEY. It's good to see you.

SAM. Yeah, you – you too.

    Beat.

    You want to bunk for an hour or so – we can go take a look
    at the city, take a stroll – what's that?

JOEY. What's what?

SAM. The church – the –

JOEY. It's St Paul's – Sam –

SAM. We should go there, we can go for a run – we can head over the bridge and grab some drinks, and take the subway.

JOEY. I'd lose my job – I really have to –

SAM. What about tomorrow?

JOEY. I don't have a day off until Sunday – we could grab a coffee then, if you're still –

SAM. When we missed you we used to shout at each other and one of us would storm out and slam and the door and scream 'screw you', you know, to pretend – and then we'd fucking piss ourselves laughing and he'd tell stories about when you were small.

(*To audience*.) She looks at the roses in her hands, she starts pulling the petals off.

(*To* JOEY.) Why won't you look at me?

JOEY. Sam, I'm really –

SAM. He told everyone about you after you left, wouldn't shut up about you. His room was fucking full of photos, the whole, time – I never knew, he used to sleep with like fifty fucking photos around his bed.

JOEY. Sam, I'm late.

SAM. I had to fucking dust those things every day.

JOEY *stands up*.

SAM *grabs her hand*.

Your mum said you hadn't spoken to her in –

JOEY. I have to go.

SAM. I love you.

JOEY. That's not the point.

SAM. How can it not be the point?

JOEY. How does it work?

SAM. What?

JOEY. How does it work, what do I *do*?

SAM. You come with me.

JOEY. What?

SAM. Come back to the States with me, make me home. I'll work for a while to get the money together and then I'll train for med school and you can find a job, there are fucking truckloads of travel magazines, and we can rent a place, and we'll cook in our fucking pyjamas – we'll get a dog, we'll drink beer and we'll – yeah – we can have a kid, and we'll make sure it only speaks to you so it sounds good, and I can teach it – I can teach it something useful – and – and – it will be amazing, it will be –

JOEY *takes* SAM's *face in her hands as if he's a little boy.*

JOEY. I don't believe you.

SAM. Why?

JOEY. Because I don't think it's going to happen that way.

SAM. It could –

JOEY. I don't think the odds are very good.

SAM. You got to try.

JOEY. I've got to work.

JOEY *stands up.*

SAM. I'll show you – two years, two more years and we'll meet here and –

JOEY. Don't, Sam, please don't do that.

SAM. For God's sake, what is wrong with you?

JOEY. Nothing.

SAM. Come with me. What have you got to lose?

JOEY. A shitty unpaid magazine job and a job in a café, a flat that I can't afford, a routine that stops me going mad, three friends that took me six months to make and stopped me feeling so lonely that I thought I was going to break in half, a lifestyle that keeps me busy enough that I don't think about the fact my dad got buried yesterday, Sam – that, that is what I have to lose. So no, I won't go running through London, I won't – dance until dawn – I won't run off to America – because you end up starstruck in a station or on a rooftop – with your mouth open, looking at the world and it feels amazing, it feels like everything is possible and it feels like just believing that, just feeling that, in your stomach is enough – but it's not enough, it's necessary but it's not enough. Because eventually you have to close your mouth, stop staring, get the fuck off the rooftop and go to work and that's what you have to believe in, you have to believe in getting up at dawn, and you have to believe in fourteen-hour shifts, you have to believe being alone is okay, you have to believe that shit magazine job might be the first step to something else. Rooftops, stars, midnight runs – they're just going to make it harder to get up in the morning.

SAM. I can't believe you've given up.

JOEY. I'm not giving up, I'm just getting started.

End of play.

HOT MESS

For Solomon

With thanks for his constancy

'Love is a fashion these days... we know how to make light of
love and how to keep our hearts at bay. I thought of myself as a
civilised woman and I discovered that I was a savage.'

Jeanette Winterson – *The Passion*

'I love you can only ever be taken to mean 'for now' – my words
were time-bound promises, a truth too disturbing for most
relationships to fully take on board.'

Alain de Botton – *Essays on Love*

'The intensity of life with somebody and the sense of it passing
has its own pathos and poignancy. There was a sense of futility
about it all disappearing into the void and I just wanted to pin
something down that would defy time, so it wouldn't all just go
off into thin air.'

Frank Auerbach – note for 'Head of E.O.W' IV.

Author's Note

Hot Mess was written in response to a series of interviews and conversations that I had with girls in their late teens and early twenties in the spring of 2010. These interviews revealed a high number of girls that claimed to enjoy and indeed demand sex with no emotional investment. It occurred to me that today's society has a paradoxical relationship with 'connection'. We are more connected than ever and yet each connection means less. *Hot Mess* questions the inherent significance of sexual practice; have we successfully socialised ourselves so that we can enjoy the act of sex separately from its emotional implications? *Hot Mess* focuses on the dialectic between those that love and those that fuck – and proposes that if casualness becomes the norm then love must be marginalised. I am fascinated by what happens to people if they are forced into those margins; I believe that this is where fundamentalism grows. If we make freaks of those that are still capable of connection, those that still believe that things can endure, then what will those people be driven to?

Production Note

Hot Mess was originally written to be performed in a nightclub, in the round. The only props used were those that would otherwise be found in this setting; glasses, straws, bottles, etc. No additional lighting or sound equipment was installed. The technical manager, the impossibly skilled Xander Macmillan, ran all the lights and sound from the DJ booth. The members of the audience could see him and each other at all times.

Music was, obviously, incredibly important to the premise of the show. We worked with the contrast between contemporary club hits and the acoustic music played by Twitch. Gwendolen Chatfield, the original Twitch, reworked club hits into acoustic pieces in order to develop this idea. We also used 'One Thousand Miles', an original piece written by Gwendolen.

The audience were seated in the round, circling the dance floor. They had their hands stamped on entry, by Polo and Jacks, one stamp saying 'HOT' the other 'MESS'. Coats were taken, money was paid – from start to finish *Hot Mess* aimed to replicate the nightclub experience.

It is, however, also possible to stage the show in a traditional theatre space. The scenes in *Hot Mess* are written as units with the intention of emphasising the fact that the story can be told in many different ways. The text, as it stands, is representative of the first staging, and all the stage directions have been included to conjure this. Subsequent directors are, of course, encouraged to start afresh.

Acknowledgements

I would like to thank Michael Whitham, Gwendolen von Einsiedel, Kerri Hall, Solomon Mousley, Ellie Chalmers and Xander Macmillan without whom this play would not have made it to the stage. I thank them for their contributions to the script and the staging and for a fun summer. It was a pleasure and a privilege to work with such a talented team and such good friends.

I would like to thank Ben Harrison, Katherine Mendelsohn and Simon Stephens for their help and tutelage whilst the script was being written.

Finally, I would like to thank Jessie Buchanan and Izzy Quilter for being impossibly tolerant, for drinking more tea and listening to more moaning than anyone should ever have to.

Ella Hickson

Hot Mess was first performed at the Hawke & Hunter Below
Stairs Nightclub, Edinburgh, on 6 August 2010, as part of the
Edinburgh Festival Fringe, with the following cast:

TWITCH	Gwendolen Chatfield
POLO	Michael Whitham
JACKS	Kerri Hall
BILLY	Solomon Mousley

Director	Ella Hickson
Technical Manager	Xander Macmillan
Producer	Eleanor Chalmers for Tantrums Ltd

Characters

TWITCH, *twenty-five, gamine – Polo's twin sister*
POLO, *twenty-five, cool and caustic – Twitch's twin brother*
JACKS, *twenty-six, well-tanned and big-breasted*
BILLY, *twenty-four, American, good-looking*

Preset

*The audience are made to queue outside of the club. On entry
they pay or hand in prepaid tickets, and have their hands
stamped by* JACKS *and* POLO. *A VIP cordon is removed by a
bouncer and they are allowed into the club. The DJ plays a
short set, contemporary club hits. The audience are free to buy
drinks from the bar and seat themselves.*

'She Said' by Plan B plays from the DJ booth. TWITCH *enters
playing acoustic guitar, she sings an acoustic version of 'She
Said'. Slowly the club version sinks away, so that only* TWITCH
can be heard. TWITCH *sings two choruses, on the second time
she reaches 'stop this crazy talk',* POLO *enters, stares at her,
smiles.* TWITCH *stops playing. Removes her guitar and places
it at the side. The club lights turn totally blue; we can hear the
sound of the sea. The twins are telling us a story.*

One

POLO. The island is small; five miles by two, no more.

TWITCH. It sits tucked into the Solent. There is one way on
and one way off.

POLO. When you come across the bridge you've got two
choices:

TWITCH. Left for Northeny – the big houses, the posh bit –

POLO. Or straight on –

TWITCH. You head on the main road into the heart of the
island, Mill Ryhthe, Sinah Warren, Mengham, the salon,

The Hut. Take West Lane and you end up in West Town
which, I suppose, makes sense and beyond all that –

POLO. Well, it's an island.

Beat.

TWITCH. There's the sea.

POLO. It comes in from every angle.

TWITCH. It keeps us calm, it holds us tight, it tucks us in.

People that live by the sea –

POLO. Walkers, talkers…

TWITCH. I used to sleep with the boat radio by my bed at night
and tune it in to the coastguard. Right through the night,
stories swam in from the sea, right into my ears. The great
adventures of –

POLO. Mayday mayday, we've found a –

TWITCH. Lifeboat men trying to save boys that thought they
were bigger than the waves.

POLO. Mayday – we've found a – off the coast of –

TWITCH. The sea. It keeps us calm, it holds us tight, it tucks us
in.

POLO. She used to say –

TWITCH. That the island would sink with all those stories.

POLO. Like the one they'd always told –

TWITCH. About Polo and me.

POLO *and* TWITCH *approach the DJ booth. They pick up a
glass each;* TWITCH *a tumbler,* POLO *a martini glass. Both
are half full with water. The water stands for the heart
throughout the scene. They chink the glasses, the lights
change, the sound of the sea stops. A new state. They take a
step forward, smile warmly at the audience. Glasses in
hands, narration begins again.*

POLO. They didn't know that they were in for a duo.

TWITCH. When they pulled him out, feet first, he bawled himself deathly 'til they cut the cord, 'til they wiped the mess and muck off him. From the second he was free: snip, wipe and wash him down – he simmered, he calmed, he sparkled – it was like the boy could only breathe when he was squeaky-clean.

POLO. They'd only banked on one; they said they'd only seen one.

TWITCH. They said I'd been hiding.

POLO. So they only got my grinner on the screen.

TWITCH. Polo was striking a pose for the ultrasound.

POLO. Sepia; even skin tone. Dream.

TWITCH. Two babies laid on scales.

POLO. A blip in the bureaucracy – there were two and they'd only planned on one.

TWITCH. Polo's clean by now so he's stopped crying.

POLO. But Twitch is still covered in –

POLO *struggles to say it – he looks at the water in his glass with disgust.*

TWITCH. – all that mess and muck. The red and the brown and the slime and the –

POLO. I'm silent and spotless.

TWITCH. I'm bawling and bloodied.

POLO. But there were two.

TWITCH. And nobody had told the heart department.

POLO. Nope.

TWITCH. Twins.

POLO. But only one heart had followed after.

POLO *pours all the water from his glass into* TWITCH*'s glass.*

TWITCH. It was the surgeon's decision: one tiny beating fluttering thing.

TWITCH *delves her hand into the water, flutters her fingers about, the water flies everywhere.*

POLO. The surgeon, heart in hand, between his finger and his thumb, the little thing, flapping there – straining to break into one chest or another; big call.

POLO *cleanly balances the martini glass between his finger and thumb.*

TWITCH. He didn't know what to do, the case was unprecedented.

POLO. Two of us there – gasping for breath –

They gasp.

– in the clean, cold white of the delivery room.

TWITCH. One was red and bawling.

POLO. The other white and silent. And the heart –

TWITCH. 'The' did you hear? 'The heart'. Not his. Not Polo's.

TWITCH *looks longingly at the full glass of water.*

Mine.

TWITCH *gulps the water greedily, it spills, it dribbles down her chin.* POLO*, meanwhile, slowly rotates his empty martini glass, a final drip falls onto the floor.*

POLO. Twitch's. She was cup-full, brimming.

POLO *turns to look at* TWITCH*, her hand over her mouth, guilty.*

TWITCH. And Polo?

POLO. Likes a fine line, a good crease and clean nails.

TWITCH. Polo Calvino was not looking to be loved.

POLO. And Twitch, his kid sister –

TWITCH. Came a thousand seconds after –

POLO. And she could do nothing but – l– (*He stumbles*.)

TWITCH. Love.

> POLO *exits*. TWITCH *kneels and plays with the water she has spilt*.

Two

TWITCH *is kneeling, spreading the spilt water into a heart shape. 'Sunny' by Bobby Hebb plays, we are on the beach. We can hear the sound of the sea, lights are soft, sunny.* BILLY *enters, the music fades.* POLO *watches*.

BILLY *walks over to* TWITCH *to try to talk to her, chickens out; walks past her.* TWITCH *sees,* TWITCH *smiles, turns to him*.

TWITCH. Hi.

BILLY. Hi.

> *Beat*.

> You're always here.

TWITCH. Um – yes, I suppose.

BILLY. You should come and hang out on the beach. The water's really warm.

TWITCH. Um – no, I –

BILLY. Oh, okay – that's fine – it doesn't matter – I –

TWITCH. I like the shade.

BILLY. What are you working on?

TWITCH. Sorry?

TWITCH steps forward, covering the heart she has drawn on the floor.

BILLY. I saw you earlier – it looked like you were drawing.

TWITCH. No.

BILLY. Sure?

TWITCH. Yeah.

BILLY. Cos you've got pen all over your finger.

TWITCH. No I haven't.

BILLY. Yes, you have.

BILLY takes her finger and shows her that it's inky. He licks his finger and rubs the ink off.

TWITCH. Oh, I was annotating my book; I star things, if I like them, underline, or –

BILLY. Right.

Still holding her finger – it's awkward for a moment. BILLY shakes her finger.

I'm Billy, by the way.

TWITCH. I'm Twitch.

BILLY. Would you like your finger back?

TWITCH. Not really.

POLO stands – Scene Three starts.

Three

Memory One.

TWITCH *and* BILLY *become puppets enacting* POLO*'s narration, expressionless.* BILLY *plays the part of all the boys mentioned in the memory scenes.*

POLO. It was troublesome from the get-go. Kicked off in kindergarten, first sign of trouble – Jimmy Trinkoff, six years old, had soiled himself and it was no fault of his own.

BILLY *as* JIMMY. Mrs Cook! Mrs Cook! I made a puddle.

POLO. He'd been taught to put his hand up if he needed to go.

BILLY *as* JIMMY. Not my fault.

POLO. Twitch had taken a shine to little Jimmy; he'd held her hand in story-time. But then he'd told her he had to go, it was time to be off, time for the little boys' room.

BILLY *and* TWITCH *put their hands up at the same time; they are stuck.*

Superglue. She'd stuck herself to him, palm to palm; took the nurse two hours to get them apart.

BILLY *and* TWITCH *stand, wrestle their hands apart.*

There was so much of it that she'd ended up having to rip little Jimmy's skin. The nurse shouted at Twitch, told her she'd done a terrible thing, told her there would be a scar, that it would be there for the rest of Jimmy's life. Wherever he went, he'd always remember our Twitch. The tears stopped, suddenly, and where the tears had been a smile spread across her pretty face.

POLO, TWITCH *and* BILLY *exit.*

Four

JACKS *enters. We are in her bedroom. She uses the audience as a mirror, adjusts her cleavage, etc. Lady Gaga plays throughout the scene, 'Poker Face' and then 'Paparazzi'.*

POLO *enters unseen.* JACKS *turns, delighted, hugs him.*

JACKS. Pooooolooooooooooo!

POLO. Kiss me – I'm old.

They hug.

They air-kiss and wipe the corners of their mouths.

JACKS. Happy bloody birthday, arse-face.

POLO. Thanks, bitch-tits.

JACKS. It's good to see you.

POLO. You got any drink?

JACKS *pulls out the front of her pants.*

JACKS. Look at this!

POLO. Uh, Jacks – my eyes just curdled!

JACKS. It's meant to be a Playboy Bunny but the ears don't look like ears, they look like – fingers, fingers flicking a freaking V – which means anyone going down there is going to think I've got a –

POLO. Hostile fanny.

JACKS. Exactly.

POLO. Is anyone here yet?

JACKS. Uh? Me.

POLO. Should have got them to trim a welcome mat in there.

JACKS. Funny.

POLO. Park-and-ride sign?

JACKS. Worst thing is it looks like I've made a fucking effort
now.

POLO. A pubic rabbit wouldn't have looked like effort?

JACKS. No, it's a logo, isn't it.

POLO. And two fingers says 'I care'?

JACKS. God, it's good to see you. You look different.

POLO. I've aged, horribly. I'm a hag.

JACKS. No you're not.

POLO. I know, I've got the skin of a twelve-year-old boy... in a
jar under my bed. Where is she?

JACKS. You're horrible! How's London?

POLO. Fine.

Beat.

JACKS. And?

POLO. And what?

JACKS. God, Polo, turn twenty-five and you turn into a total
fucking buzz-kill, eh?

POLO. I've been ringing her all day but I haven't heard a thing.

JACKS. Fuck Uncle Fester. She'll turn up – she always does.
Tonight it's you and me – the power team, reunited. We're
like LiLo and that lezzer, Paris and Nicole, Cheryl and –

POLO. Laurel and Hardly.

JACKS. – Dannii.

POLO. Susan Boyle and her cat Pebbles.

JACKS. It's your fucking birthday!

POLO. Halfway to fifty. Where is she? You'd think she'd want to be on time.

JACKS. Oh God, it's so fucking good to see you!

POLO. Come on then, Jacqueline! Get some bloody crotch-swatches out. It's not a celebration unless half the island can see your ovaries!

JACKS. Waaaa! Guess what?

POLO. What?

JACKS. Caroline Granger, Meg Watson, Sophie Cooper.

POLO. Dream team. Not.

JACKS. Married.

POLO. Fuck me. Who the hell married Meg Watson and that mole?

JACKS. Nick Hastings. They've got a kid.

POLO. God, that's got to be one fucking ugly baby.

JACKS. It got the mole 'n' all. Meg brings it into the salon to get the little hairs removed, makes me want to puke.

POLO. Vomit stations.

JACKS. It's been a bit horrible, Polo.

POLO. I bet, I hate all the lying that's involved with an ugly baby and then they want you to touch it and put your face really close to it and it's all too –

JACKS. No. It's all been a bit horrible; without you.

POLO. Chica.

JACKS. Everyone's sold out, it's like the island's got smaller. The only thing there's any more of is rust.

Beat.

POLO. Which I see you've been bathing in?

JACKS. What?

POLO. You look like a Dorito.

JACKS. What? No I don't. I've just caught the sun.

POLO. You've caught something! It looks like you've been using HP for hand cream.

JACKS. Fuck off, dough-boy.

POLO. Pumpkin.

JACKS. Fish-flesh.

POLO. Basketball.

JACKS. Polar bear.

POLO. Tangerine.

JACKS. Ice queen.

POLO. Wotsit.

JACKS. Prawn cracker.

POLO. Yoke.

JACKS (*slow*). Yogurt-body. Coconut, marshmallow, Michelin Man.

POLO (*with aggression*). Neon cunting whore!

Silence descends for several seconds.

Come on! It's fucking party time!

JACKS. We'll do it like we used to. We'll get shit-faced, we'll drink 'til we can't stand and dance, dance 'til everything spins –

POLO. And they'll all be watching.

JACKS. Every set of eyes in the place – dragging on us –

POLO. Like tide round a –

JACKS. Buoy.

POLO. A good-looking boy!

JACKS. A perfect-looking boy!

POLO. Eyes like cameras.

JACKS. Each blink like a paparazzi snap.

POLO (*repeats as an echo*). 'Papa – papa – papa –'

JACKS. 'That's Polo and Jacks.'

POLO (*repeats as an echo*). 'That's Polo and Jacks.'

JACKS. 'Fuck me – she's hot!'

POLO. 'Fuck me – he's dreamy.'

JACKS. 'If only I could nail a girl like that.' Clawing at my pants they'll be – biting at the bit.

POLO. Your bits.

JACKS. You'll pick me a good one.

POLO. Tall, not too tall, well-built, charming not clever. Looks good, seems good, sounds good.

JACKS. Just enough to make me want to –

POLO. But not too much, can't have you falling.

JACKS. I'm no limp dick.

POLO. Course not.

JACKS. I snare him.

POLO. You fuck him – toilet, beach, bed, who cares, don't ask for his name.

JACKS. I won't give him mine if he asks.

POLO. You're done.

JACKS. I cum.

POLO. You leave.

JACKS. You laugh. I walk away feeling –

POLO. Powerful.

JACKS. Untouchable.

POLO. He –

JACKS. He?

POLO. Sees us high-five.

They high-five.

JACKS. He frowns.

POLO. Not sure he understands.

JACKS. Not sure he wants to understand.

POLO. Little boy blows out his chest and tries to stand like a man.

JACKS. You laugh!

POLO. You laugh! He looks like he might cry.

JACKS. We gave him one for womankind!

POLO. And so and so and so we drink until we go blind!

They laugh.

Beat.

JACKS. Polo?

POLO. Hm?

JACKS. New dresses didn't feel like new dresses when you weren't here.

Beat.

POLO. Have you got anything to drink?

JACKS. Downstairs, but don't go – we'll go later, when the taxi arrives.

POLO. I'm parched.

POLO *goes to leave.* JACKS *flinches and grabs him.*

JACKS. No.

POLO. Why?

JACKS. Don't.

POLO. I'm just going to say hi.

JACKS. Stay here. Please.

POLO. Why?

JACKS. She'll be washing up.

POLO. So?

JACKS. Stay!

POLO. Jacks?

JACKS. We're having fun!

POLO. Jacks. Get a grip – I'll be back in two minutes.

JACKS. She splashes around in the water because it covers the sound of her sniffing, but she forgets to wipe her face before she turns around, so she'll turn and grin at you, but she'll have red eyes and black tracks of mascara down her cheeks.

Beat.

Dad's gone.

POLO. Right.

Beat.

JACKS. Mum's a fucking buzz-kill these days.

POLO. When?

JACKS. About a year ago – just after you left.

POLO. And she's still blubbing?

JACKS. Yeah.

POLO. Fucking hell.

JACKS. Dad's pumping chicks left, right and centre – he's got it made. I just don't know what Mum thinks she's winning by not getting over it.

Beat.

POLO. Fairy-soft hands?

JACKS. Maybe.

POLO. Nobody likes a party pooper.

Beat.

JACKS. I can't bear to look at her before a night out. It makes me feel a bit sick.

POLO. Have you rung her?

JACKS. Who?

POLO. Twitch. She's nearly an hour late, we should ring her.

JACKS. Right.

POLO. I'm going downstairs to get a drink.

POLO exits. JACKS stands a moment, exits.

Five

TWITCH *grabs* BILLY *and drags him on stage. We can hear the sound of the sea. 'Sunny' by Bobby Hebb plays, lights are soft, we are on the beach.* TWITCH *talks to the audience unless otherwise indicated.* BILLY *is unaware of the audience throughout the scene.* POLO *watches.*

TWITCH. He has green eyes. When he gets out of the sea –

TWITCH *pours a glass of water over* BILLY*'s head; she rubs it through his hair. He shakes it off and dries himself on her T-shirt.*

I look at him and the water has stuck his eyelashes together in clumps. As they dry, the salt crystallises on the ends. It looks like he has tens of tiny magic wands where his eye-lashes should be. Alacazam.

TWITCH *runs away from* BILLY; *he catches her, tucks her head under his arm.*

He's big enough that I fit into the crook of his arm. I rest my head on his chest – (*Does so.*) in one ear I can hear his heart and in the other, I can hear the sound of the sea.

The sound of the sea fades. They are in TWITCH's *bedroom.* BILLY *pulls* TWITCH *down onto the floor; she rests on his chest and tries to speak to him. He's tired, he tries to sleep.*

(*To* BILLY.) When I was small –

BILLY. Hm?

TWITCH (*to* BILLY). I'd leave the window open when I went to sleep; I'd close my eyes and listen – I'd imagine that the waves were tucking me in.

BILLY. You're such a geek.

TWITCH (*to* BILLY). Oi. (*Beat.*) Don't you think afternoon sun is a special kind of sun?

BILLY. What?

TWITCH (*to* BILLY). The way it looks like lemonade on the duvet.

BILLY *tries to make* TWITCH *hush; he smothers her in a hug. She laughs, wriggles out and away from him, he curls, he sleeps.*

He sleeps, curled, comma-shaped – it looks like a comfortable alien has landed. I imagine that this might be the beginning of our story.

TWITCH *picks up her guitar and begins to play an acoustic version of 'Sex on Fire' by Kings of Leon. She sings initially to the sleeping* BILLY *and then to the audience; she builds complicity with them, she's mischievous, fun.*

TWITCH *stops singing, puts her guitar down. In hushes she begins to talk again.* BILLY *sleeps.*

Imagine ten years' time, kitchen table, friends. He catches my thigh as I walk from the door, holds me to him and laughs. (*Does an impression of* BILLY, *older.*) 'How did we meet? Ink, finger – you know. Long story.' His palm rises casually up my bum cheek onto my waist, friends look jealous. I smile – you should be. (*Back as* BILLY.) 'We didn't think it was going anywhere – God no, it was a fling, a flirtation, a sojourn, but there was nothing we could do; it was – unavoidable, necessary. We just fell.'

TWITCH *climbs back into bed alongside* BILLY. BILLY *rouses.*

BILLY. What you thinking?

TWITCH (*to* BILLY). Nothing.

BILLY *jumps up and straddles her.*

BILLY. You have an awesomely flat stomach. It's like the – Sahara.

TWITCH (*to* BILLY). That's quite hilly.

BILLY. Holland.

TWITCH (*to* BILLY). I guess. (*To audience.*) He looks up at me from my stomach. (*To* BILLY.) Hi chum.

BILLY. Hey dude.

TWITCH. He looks like a toddler. He's pretending his finger is stuck in my belly button.

BILLY (*speaks into an imaginary walkie-talkie*). Tsch, tsch... Billy to base camp! Tsch... Billy to base camp! I've fallen down a pretty killer ravine here, guys!

TWITCH. I look at his face. I like his face. I kiss his face.

They kiss.

BILLY. Base camp, base camp we've discovered – a –

TWITCH. A...?

BILLY. A...

BILLY pushes himself up, thumps his chest – he pretends to be a gorilla. He nearly falls on TWITCH, *she laughs.*

TWITCH (*to* BILLY). If we're going to have sex you're going to have to stop pretending to be King Kong.

BILLY. Bear Grylls?

TWITCH (*to* BILLY). Nope.

BILLY. Indiana Jones?

TWITCH (*to* BILLY). Definitely not!

BILLY. Attenborough?

TWITCH (*to* BILLY). Hmm?

BILLY. Oh really?

They laugh, they quiet.

I like you.

TWITCH. I like you too.

They kiss.

Six

Memory Two.

We snap into memory lighting. POLO *stands.* BILLY *and* TWITCH *become puppets.*

POLO. Twitch is thirteen, Mrs Black's art class. There'd been rumours of her being a prodigy.

TWITCH *mimes painting.*

Mrs Black was impossibly excited about the unveiling of Twitch's long-awaited pastoral scenes. The Powells were our next-door neighbours. Two kids; Sarah – a snotty thing – Nick, Twitch's age.

BILLY *as* NICK *presents himself.*

Good-looking boy. There'd been some kissing I believe.

BILLY *as* NICK *and* TWITCH *stand apart and snog the air, tongues out.*

Mrs Black ordered the unveiling –

TWITCH *unveils the painting.* BILLY *as* NICK *looks horrified.*

– and Mum was nearly sick on her suedes. Thirteen-year-old Nick Powell sees fifteen finely drawn images of his own face, inter-spliced with photos taken from his next-door neighbour's top window. She'd caught him every which way, flexing, picking, fiddling, sleeping: it was all there, one big visual quilt of surveillance. In all the fuss Nick splits and Twitch slips. Her pen finds itself lodged in the deep tissue of Nick Powell's forearm. A small blue dot; hard as they tried to wash it off, they couldn't shift it. A tattoo, you might say.

TWITCH *and* POLO *exit.* BILLY *stands frozen until activated by* JACKS*' entry.*

Seven

BILLY *stands.* JACKS *enters, ready for a night out. We are back in* JACKS*' house, Lady Gaga plays.*

JACKS. Where the fuck have you been, Captain bloody America?

BILLY. I'm sorry, I got held up.

JACKS. Polo wants to go.

BILLY. So glory boy's arrived then?

JACKS. We were meant to leave half a bloody hour ago, the queue's going to be huge by the time we get there.

BILLY. What's with the name?

JACKS. What?

BILLY. 'Polo' – it's a weird fucking name?

JACKS. Hold up, Watson. Isn't your sister called yogurt?

BILLY. Yogi.

JACKS. Bet she can't bear it.

JACKS *laughs at her own joke.* BILLY *grimaces.*

Born with a hole in the middle.

BILLY. What?

JACKS. Hole in his heart. They say they used a bit of Twitch to patch him up – but I'm pretty sure they just whopped the beater right out of him.

BILLY. Shut up.

JACKS. Seriously, the boy's a tin man.

BILLY. You can't live without a heart.

JACKS. Polo can.

BILLY. He sounds like a really nice guy.

JACKS. He's the best of men.

BILLY. You mind if I have a shower?

JACKS. You haven't got time.

BILLY. I'll be really quick.

JACKS. No, Billy – I want you to meet Polo. Come on.

BILLY. Um, Jacks?

JACKS. Come on.

BILLY. I, uh – you know, you know that I'm not – we're not – I'm not your boyfriend.

JACKS. No! (*Laughs, loudly, sees that* BILLY *is earnest and becomes serious*.) No, no Billy, I know.

BILLY. Right, just because… you know, we had been… sleeping together and I didn't want you to…

JACKS. What? Order a table for two at Pizza Hut?

BILLY. Get hurt.

JACKS. Billy, trust that I would let you know if you were my boyfriend.

Beat.

BILLY. Right, sure.

JACKS. Just hurry the fuck up, alright?

BILLY. Yep, yes I will. Sorry I –

BILLY *turns to go.*

JACKS. Billy?

BILLY. Yeah?

JACKS. Don't make me out to be a limp dick, alright?

BILLY. No.

JACKS. It was jokes.

BILLY. Good jokes.

JACKS. Side-splitters. Now, hurry the fuck up, we're late!

JACKS *and* BILLY *faux-box for several punches, smile;* JACKS *exits –* BILLY *watches her go, a little uncomfortably, then turns. He is startled by* POLO, *who has been standing, watching.*

BILLY. Oh hey, mate – I'm Billy.

BILLY *offers his hand.*

POLO *ignores his hand.*

POLO. Polo.

BILLY. Yeah… I know. Jacks is your biggest fan. She hasn't stopped talking about you for weeks.

POLO. She didn't mention you.

BILLY. Right – well – I'm Billy and… I'm just going to grab a shower.

POLO. Are you living here?

BILLY. Just for the summer. Our parents are friends.

POLO. You're American?

BILLY. Yes.

POLO. Are you coming with us?

BILLY. I think so – Jacks said it was – uh, apologies, dude; I should have said, uh – happy birthday, man.

POLO. We're quite late.

BILLY. Sure, I'll be real quick. Twitch is on her way so we can head straight out when I'm done.

POLO. What?

BILLY. I'll be real quick –

POLO. Twitch?

BILLY. Hm?

POLO. You said Twitch?

BILLY. I bumped into her on my way – she said she was –

POLO. 'Bumped'?

BILLY. On the road.

POLO. Which road?

BILLY. The road.

POLO. Which road?

BILLY. I don't remember the name.

POLO. The island's very small.

BILLY. Sure – but –

POLO. Five miles by two – no more.

BILLY. All the same, I don't remember the name of the road.

Long pause.

Anyway – I should grab that shower.

POLO. She won't be long.

BILLY. No, I'm sure she won't. It was a pleasure –

POLO. Hm.

POLO *watches* BILLY *go.*

Eight

POLO *stands from Scene Seven,* TWITCH *enters unseen. They speak slowly; their mode is unnerving. We are still in* JACKS' *house, the hallway now; Lady Gaga has thinned to silence.*

TWITCH. Hello, Polo.

POLO. Sproggit.

Long pause.

Where have you been?

TWITCH. Where have you been?

POLO. You're late.

TWITCH. You're late.

POLO. Jacks said seven.

TWITCH. You're a year late.

Beat.

Have you missed me?

POLO. Twitch?

TWITCH. Thank you for calling.

POLO. I always asked Mum and Dad –

TWITCH. How I was? It's not quite the same though, is it, Angel-face?

POLO. No.

TWITCH. Well then.

POLO. Please don't be angry.

TWITCH. Why not?

POLO. I'm not used to it. You've never been –

TWITCH. You never left before.

POLO. I never came back before.

TWITCH. Because you never left before.

POLO. But now I'm back.

TWITCH. Why did you go?

Beat.

POLO. Dad said you're doing photography.

TWITCH. Yes.

POLO. What you snapping?

TWITCH. Things.

POLO. Twitch?

TWITCH. Pictures.

POLO. Fine.

TWITCH. I'm angry.

POLO. I can tell.

TWITCH. Tideline.

POLO. Seaweed?

TWITCH. It's rising.

POLO. Greenpeace, hippy shit?

TWITCH. Our kids won't play on the same sand we played on.

POLO. Sand moves anyway.

TWITCH. The island's disappearing.

POLO. Right. Will you kiss me?

> POLO *steps forward*. TWITCH *steps back*.

TWITCH. Right?

POLO. To say hello. It's been for ever.

> POLO *steps forward*. TWITCH *steps back*.

TWITCH. Just – 'right'? Don't you find that – unbearable? That our memories are tied to things that will be under the water by the time our children are born.

POLO. Yours.

TWITCH. No; ours, our memories, Polo, where we grew up.

POLO. Yours. Your children.

> *Long pause.*

TWITCH. Happy birthday, Polo.

POLO. Not 'til midnight.

TWITCH. Twenty-five.

POLO. Quarter century.

TWITCH. We're getting older. I sometimes thought we might not.

POLO. Yes.

TWITCH. But we are.

POLO. We should go, can't be late. We'll be on our way to fifty before we start drinking.

TWITCH. Polo?

POLO. What?

Long pause.

TWITCH. There's a boy –

POLO *says nothing.* TWITCH *moves closer. Close enough to touch him, she raises her hand to almost touch his cheek.*

Polo – there's a –

POLO (*jolts his head away, they do not touch*). Come on!

POLO *leaves.* TWITCH *is left standing for several seconds.* TWITCH *exits.*

Nine

We are back on the beach. It is night now. We can hear the sound of the sea, the revellers walk in a line towards the club. POLO *leads.* POLO *and* TWITCH *talk to the audience,* BILLY *and* JACKS *remain in the scene.*

POLO. I wanted to get to The Hut by walking along the seafront, along the line of the tide, I just wanted to put my feet on the last bits of sand that were dry before the waves came in.

BILLY. Isn't it weird –?

TWITCH. What?

BILLY. Isn't it weird –

TWITCH. What?

BILLY. Isn't it weird –

TWITCH. What?

BILLY. Isn't it weird when it's dark and still hot – you can taste the salt in the air.

TWITCH puts her finger in the air and then into BILLY's mouth. He sucks it. JACKS appears, bringing up the rear.

JACKS. Polo!

The four characters take up static positions at intervals across the stage.

TWITCH. We're walking in a line, Polo up front; strangely quiet. Jacks keeps screaming –

JACKS. Polo! Tell us a joke – I want to hear a joke, Polo!

TWITCH. He doesn't say a word. Behind him, Billy, I stare at the space on the back of his head where I laid my hand this afternoon, whilst he slept.

JACKS. Polo – tell us a joke!

POLO. Billy pulls out a little plastic packet from his back pocket and passes it down the line. The taste is so familiar it might as well be milk and fucking cookies.

The four take pills from their pockets and swallow them down.

TWITCH. The tide is rising.

POLO. Nipping at your heels.

TWITCH. The sky is sweating stars. I look at Billy and the moon is making his face shine white, he looks beautiful.

POLO. Two moons – one in the sky, bright white – the other, its twin, is reflected in the water – you can barely see him.

TWITCH. I've always had this idea that when the tide rises around an island it means that there is less land to stand on –

JACKS. Polo! Tell us a bloody joke!

TWITCH. Which means that with each wave people must be moving closer together.

TWITCH *and* BILLY *kiss.* POLO *looks on.*

POLO. I'm not sure I can breathe.

Ten

'She Said' by Plan B plays. DJ emerges from behind his decks and becomes a nightclub attendant. JACKS, *at the back of the queue, rushes forward, pushing* BILLY, POLO *and* TWITCH. JACKS *turns and berates the imaginary queue barger behind her. The four characters pay the attendant, get their hands stamped, and give him their coats. He returns behind the decks. The four characters enter the club. They dance, they drink, they look at the audience as if they are also on the dance floor.* POLO *does not take his eyes off* TWITCH. TWITCH *watches* BILLY.

TWITCH. I keep pretending to wipe my nose with the cuff of my shirt; he used it today to dry his hair after we came out of the sea. The smell of him, skin, salt, sweat; I trace an exact line from where he is standing to where I am. Yes, that man, there, with the chequered shirt, by the bar – yes, him, making the bar girl laugh – 'Yes he is rather isn't he? Thank you – I know.'

I wonder if any other two people in this bar have had sex today. I like that I know, I can still feel, in my knickers – I look at the way he smiles and talks with other people and only I know what the underside of his penis looks like. It makes me smile. My secret, my man, I want to belong to him, to be his; be my boy for a thousand years.

POLO *clicks, snap into memory state.* TWITCH *and* BILLY *freeze.*

Eleven

Memory Three

TWITCH *and* BILLY *become puppets once again. They stand opposite each other;* BILLY *has a beer bottle in his hand.*

POLO. Peter Harris, sixteen years old, behind the bike shed of the Island Academy. It was the day before the school disco. I'd spent two weeks looking for the right dress for her, the right shoes, the right hairband.

We'd even gone to the trouble of organising a little choreography for the most probable hits of school disco 2002. 'It's getting hot in here'; chicken neck, chicken neck, beep, beep, chicken neck, chicken neck, beep.

But the day before the big night, little Pedro wanted a trial run; first boy to find his hand in our Twitch's knickers.

Pretended not to know her the next night, wouldn't even talk to her, said he couldn't remember her name. Who forgets a name like Twitch? Electrical mishap –

POLO *clicks. Blackout.*

– speakers wired funny they said, no one was quite sure what had happened. Little Peter was standing too close to the sound system – it certainly was getting hot in there –

Electric blue lights flash, back to blackout.

– two hundred and thirty volts, saw our Petey flying through the air – quite the spectacle, turned his hair into the short and curlies that he'd so enjoyed exploring the day before. And try as they might, they just couldn't make it straight again.

POLO, BILLY *and* TWITCH *stay frozen until* JACKS *arrives.*

Twelve

'Hot in Herre' by Nelly plays. JACKS enters, we are back in the club. '(I've Had) The Time of My Life' by Bill Medley and Jennifer Warnes begins to play.

JACKS. Polo! Let's do the lift!

BILLY, POLO *and* TWITCH *snap round, horrified.*

POLO. Jacks – no!

JACKS *jumps into the air.* BILLY *appears, seemingly from nowhere, and catches her.*

BILLY. Jacks, no! That is not a good idea!

JACKS. We used to do this all the time.

TWITCH. We were quite a lot smaller then –

JACKS *(wriggles free from* BILLY*).* Don't call me fat!

TWITCH. Stop shouting. I wasn't calling you fat.

JACKS. It's fine!

BILLY. Guys – people are kind of –

TWITCH. People are looking.

JACKS. It's fine!

POLO. I can't do it.

JACKS. It's like riding a bike.

POLO. I have literally no upper-body strength any more.

BILLY. Of course you do.

POLO. I don't.

BILLY. You must have.

JACKS. It has to be you, Polo, like old times! Okay – I'm
coming –

POLO. Jacks – no! This is a bad idea.

JACKS. It's fine – it will be fine. You'll remember how –

POLO. No, Jacks! We're different, you're not Baby any more,
I'm not Johnny any more.

BILLY. You were Johnny?

POLO. Yes.

TWITCH. He's actually dead now.

POLO. Why can't you imagine me as Johnny?

BILLY. I don't know.

JACKS. Say the line, Polo – Polo, say the line –

POLO. Bigot.

TWITCH. Polo?

POLO. What?

JACKS. Come on!

BILLY. Swayze is like a stallion.

TWITCH. Was. He's dead.

BILLY. He was a stallion.

POLO. What's your point, monkey boy?

JACKS. Polo, say the line and I'll run!

BILLY. You must, like, wank? That's forearm strength.

TWITCH. Billy, leave him.

POLO. I'm fine.

BILLY. He doesn't wank?

JACKS. Polo!

POLO. You can speak to me, you can ask me – I can hear you.

BILLY. You don't wank?

TWITCH. Billy – stop it.

POLO (*turns sharply away*). Jacks! Come on!

JACKS. I'm ready!

BILLY. You don't wank? He doesn't wank?

TWITCH. Billy, stop it. Jacks, stop!

JACKS. Shut your trap, Uncle Fester – I'm coming – say the line –

BILLY. You know that's fucked up?

TWITCH. Billy! Jacks!

JACKS. I'm coming!

BILLY. Dude? You don't wank?

JACKS. I'm coming! Polo!

BILLY. What the fuck are you?

POLO (*screams uncomfortably loud*). Nobody puts Baby in the corner!

JACKS starts screaming and running towards POLO, POLO stands with his arms out, ready to catch her. The music rises to a crescendo, at the point of flight – blackout.

Thirteen

Lights up. JACKS and POLO freeze. JACKS is sprawled, face down on the floor of the club, her head stuck under the DJ booth. POLO stands, hands over his mouth. BILLY and TWITCH sit on the bar/sea wall. We are on the beach.

TWITCH. Oh my God.

BILLY. That was hilarious.

TWITCH. Don't – don't laugh –

BILLY. Man, she just fucking face-planted in the middle of the bar.

TWITCH. Polo just stood there.

BILLY. He saw these huge tits coming towards him and he just couldn't move.

TWITCH. He just stood there.

BILLY. Tit-ma-tised!

Lights down on BILLY *and* TWITCH.

Fourteen

Snap back to the dance floor. Lights up on POLO *and* JACKS, JACKS *starts moaning in pain,* POLO *begins to shift about anxiously.*

JACKS. Polo, I think I'm stuck.

POLO. Get up!

JACKS gets up slowly, faces the crowd, is mortified and tries to retreat back to the floor.

Come on; just act natural!

JACKS. Everybody's looking.

JACKS and POLO smile weakly, dance weakly.

Natural? I just wiped out in the middle of the –

POLO. Where's Twitch gone?

Looks manically across the crowd.

JACKS. Polo, everybody's staring at me.

POLO. Where is she?

JACKS. Polo, everybody's staring.

POLO. Jacks?

JACKS. Polo.

POLO (*grabs her with both hands*). Twitch?

JACKS. I think she fucked off to fuck Billy.

> JACKS *totally absorbed by the eyes that are on her – starts to wave, wink. She sees the audience, sees that they are looking at her.*

POLO. Where?

JACKS. Looked like they were headed to the beach.

POLO. What?

JACKS. Sandy number, organ grinder. Now – look –

POLO. Right.

JACKS. Look; look, at them looking. Everybody is staring.

> POLO *looks up, around the club.* POLO *sees the audience.*

POLO. You're right.

> *Lights drop on* POLO *and* JACKS. *Lights come up on the audience.*

It must be because you're so hot, Jacks.

> *They walk slowly towards the audience, maintaining eye contact – they walk back again.*

JACKS. They can't stop looking. (*Beat.*) Look at him.

POLO. Where?

JACKS. Having to sit on his fucking hands.

POLO (*laughs*). Practically fucking dribbling.

JACKS (*to the selected audience member*). You like it? You
    want to touch it?

POLO. Go over to him. Give him a real show.

JACKS. You reckon?

POLO. Teach him a lesson.

JACKS. Look at him, he literally can't look away.

POLO. Touch him.

JACKS. Shut up!

POLO. Touch him!

> JACKS *touches the audience member.* JACKS *and* POLO
> *squeal with laughter –*

JACKS. He's gone red – he's gone bright fucking –

POLO. Over there?

JACKS. Which one?

> POLO *points to another member of the audience.*

POLO. There.

JACKS. Ha.

POLO. He's trying to look away – doesn't know where to look.

JACKS. Got to keep his eyes on this, can't help himself, can
    you, big boy?

POLO. Dance for him.

JACKS. I'm dancing.

POLO. Make him fucking squirm. Make him beg – he wants to
    watch, give him something to fucking look at!

> JACKS *goes right over, dances provocatively.* JACKS *and*
> POLO *squeal with laugher.*

Him – over there, geek chic with the glasses.

JACKS. His eyes drag –

POLO. Like tide –

JACKS. On –

POLO. You.

They laugh sardonically.

Take something off.

JACKS. You reckon?

POLO. Look at them, it's pathetic – little bit of human fucking flesh and they can't keep their eyes off.

JACKS. Looky looky.

POLO. Licky licky.

JACKS. Can't stop staring!

POLO. Take something off.

JACKS. You want to see – you want a show?

POLO. You want to see a real show?

POLO *rips off* JACKS' *jacket.*

JACKS. He's shitting himself!

POLO. Careful the wife doesn't spot that trouser tent, sir.

JACKS. Come on, booooys!!

POLO. They're going wild for it!

JACKS. Like little fucking puppies. This is so funny!

POLO. They're shouting your name, Jacks – give them what they want!

JACKS *tentatively goes to take her top off,* POLO *eggs her on.* JACKS, *excited by* POLO, *pulls her top off, leaving her bra on.*

JACKS (*squeals*). That was so funny! I can't believe I just did that!

POLO. Jacks, people are coming in off the beach!

POLO *stands behind* JACKS *and angles her towards male members of the audience. From hereon in he shouts right into her ear.*

JACKS. What are they saying? What's a 'tizau'?

POLO. 'Get your tits out!'

JACKS (*reels with laughter, screaming*). Everybody wants me!

POLO. Get your tits out!

JACKS. They're all taking pictures!

POLO. You're a celeb, Jacks!

POLO *pushes* JACKS *forward aggressively towards the audience.*

JACKS. Polo! Take a picture of them taking pictures of me!

POLO. You're so fucking fierce!

JACKS. They can't get enough!

POLO. Get your tits out!

JACKS (*screams*). I feel invincible!

POLO (*screams*). Get your fucking tits out!

JACKS *takes her top off. Blackout.* JACKS *exits.*

Fifteen

POLO *stands centre stage, the blackout remains.*

POLO. I was sitting in a café and a woman got out one of her
    breasts and pushed her thick nipple into her baby's mouth
    and I retched. (*Beat.*) You're gorgeous, you're fabulous,
    you're amazing – PS, if I had to actually look at what's
    between your legs I'd – (*Beat.*) When a pregnant woman
    passes me in the street I have to look away.

POLO *retreats.*

Sixteen

Lights pull back up on BILLY *and* TWITCH, *still seated on the
bar/sea wall. We hear sounds of the sea. We are on the beach.*
BILLY *jumps down off the bar/sea wall and helps* TWITCH
down. They walk across the dance floor as if it were a beach.
POLO *looks on.*

BILLY. Polo really doesn't wank or – ?

TWITCH. No.

BILLY. That's fucked up, man.

TWITCH. I don't know.

BILLY. What?

TWITCH. It makes sense to me sometimes.

BILLY. Why?

TWITCH. It might be easier.

BILLY. I'd fucking explode.

TWITCH. Really?

BILLY. Well, you know –

Long pause, they wander.

TWITCH. Billy, how many people have you slept with?

BILLY. Hm?

TWITCH. Roughly?

BILLY. Oh, I don't know –

TWITCH. Roughly?

BILLY. Fucking look at that moon, man, it's incredible, it's so big and –

TWITCH. Billy?

BILLY. Hm?

TWITCH. How many?

BILLY. How many what?

TWITCH. Tell me.

BILLY. You?

TWITCH. Two. You're the second.

BILLY. Oh.

TWITCH. What?

BILLY. Nothing, I just. I don't know, that's not very many. Are your family like… religious or… unattractive? That was a joke. I was joking.

TWITCH. Neither.

BILLY. Right.

TWITCH. I'm just aware of my – I've learnt –

BILLY. What?

TWITCH. I don't have much of a capacity for casual sex.

Beat.

BILLY. Right.

TWITCH. It's natural.

BILLY. Hm?

TWITCH. Jacks, Jacks always calls me Uncle Fester because Uncle Fester's a freak, you know, from the –

BILLY. *The Addams Family.*

TWITCH. Yeah, them.

BILLY. A freak?

TWITCH. But since I started having sex.

BILLY. Just that once before –

TWITCH. You.

BILLY. Mm-hm.

TWITCH. I've read loads.

BILLY. Read?

TWITCH. Did you ever get told the story about teeth at school?

BILLY. Teeth?

TWITCH. About how you should imagine that your teeth had no enamel. (*Speaks with mouth open, imitating.*) Imagine that the roots were thirty-two tiny fishing lines, totally exposed, sensitive to the slightest touch –

BILLY. Ouch.

TWITCH. Then you gulp a big glass of water.

BILLY. Man, stop, it's horrible.

TWITCH. And all the fishing rods are waving in the –

BILLY. Stop it!

TWITCH. The enamel was trust or marriage or –

BILLY. Say again?

TWITCH. Armour.

BILLY. Armour?

TWITCH. You shouldn't go eating apples without enamel on your teeth.

BILLY. You lost me.

TWITCH. I get very – attached. I have trouble... letting go.

BILLY. Oh.

TWITCH. What I'm saying is, that it's Jacks that should be called Uncle Fester.

BILLY. Why?

TWITCH. For her it's all so –

BILLY. What?

TWITCH. I don't know... it doesn't... Do you fancy her? I mean, would you ever – ?

BILLY. Twitch – I – um –

TWITCH. I find it – incredible how she can sleep with people and it doesn't mean a thing.

Beat.

BILLY. I think that's pretty normal, or it's, it's you know, just being – adult.

TWITCH. Do you think you can choose?

BILLY. What?

TWITCH. What kind of heart you have?

BILLY. Yes.

Beat.

TWITCH. You know there's a hormone called oxytocin and it triggers the feeling of attachment. During sex, women produce around ten times more of it than men.

BILLY. Right.

TWITCH. And for the men, testosterone suppresses the oxytocin, so they are wired to be less attached. When men ejaculate they release prolactin instead, it makes them less risk-averse – they want to skydive and women want to cuddle.

BILLY. You know your stuff.

TWITCH. I've read.

BILLY. Clearly.

TWITCH. We're wired to want you to stay.

BILLY. But not all girls –

TWITCH. I think they're working against their wiring.

BILLY. Right.

TWITCH. I'm normal.

BILLY. Good to know.

TWITCH. Normal.

BILLY. You said.

TWITCH. Just saying.

BILLY. I'm not sure it needs repeating.

TWITCH. I'm sorry. It's just when I said the 'two people' thing –

BILLY. You don't need to justify –

TWITCH. I did. You looked scared.

BILLY. I wasn't scared – I just –

TWITCH. How many people have you – ?

BILLY. It's not the same –

TWITCH. I don't mind.

BILLY. I mean, I'd put my dick places I wouldn't put my fingers.

Beat.

TWITCH. Right.

BILLY. Not that – that doesn't mean –

TWITCH. It's fine.

BILLY. I like you.

TWITCH. I like you too.

BILLY *smiles.*

I wish there was a word in between.

BILLY. In between – ?

TWITCH. Like and –

Beat.

There's a gap.

BILLY. 'There's a gap'?

TWITCH. The gap. They say that's what really what makes people fall in – that there's a gap between men and women. A space in between what they mean – like a – and it can't quite be crossed because their languages build different bridges and the bridges never quite meet – and that, that – sex is like this thing between the bridges, like a dictionary, like translation, and when people fall – it means that they've jumped off their bridges.

BILLY. I don't get it.

TWITCH. I think that's the point.

BILLY. What?

TWITCH. You're not meant to get it, because I said it.

BILLY. What's the point in the story if I don't get it?

TWITCH. The point of the story is that you don't get it.

BILLY. I'm not sure I understand.

TWITCH. Exactly.

BILLY. Really?

TWITCH. Yes.

BILLY. Yes.

TWITCH. Right.

BILLY. Right. Okay.

Beat.

TWITCH. Billy, I love you.

Beat.

BILLY. Twitch, I'm leaving.

Lights fade out. BILLY *and* TWITCH *sit. We can only hear the sound of the sea.*

Seventeen

BILLY *and* TWITCH *sit silently on the beach.* JACKS *enters and stands nearby.* POLO *looks on.*

JACKS. I –

TWITCH. Sea.

JACKS. Him, across the bar.

TWITCH. We sit in silence.

JACKS. Never seem him before. He's hot. He –

TWITCH. Waves.

JACKS. His eyes drag on me like –

TWITCH. Tide.

JACKS. The club is thumping.

TWITCH. The water is calm.

JACKS. He comes over –

TWITCH. He's quiet. I can tell he feels the weight of my words, the responsibility sits like stones. Two silent silhouettes on the –

JACKS. Hi. Hi. Drink. You want to? Alright – are you – ?

TWITCH. Shore.

JACKS. Alright then.

TWITCH. It's funny how my love feels so heavy to him when his muscles are so much bigger than mine.

JACKS. He drags me – his eyes –

TWITCH. The tide is coming in. We sit on the last bit of –

JACKS. Land, on me. They stick to me. He wants what I've got and it feels like power.

TWITCH. I feel totally powerless.

JACKS. He pushes me into the cubicle. He locks the door behind him. The toilet lid is cold against the back of my thighs.

TWITCH. Kiss me.

JACKS. Fuck me.

TWITCH. I am close enough to see the tiny blacks of his pupils. My fingertips map his face in the dark.

JACKS. The neon light flickers over his head – it looks like camera snaps for the –

TWITCH. Stars. The sky is sweating stars.

JACKS. It's hot. It's so fucking hot.

TWITCH. The only thing I can hear is the sea. His big man hands falter over my waistband.

JACKS. He pushes himself between my thighs and I tell him to slow down. Apply myself to his belt buckle. He slows, he waits, bated fucking breath for me to give him what he wants. (*Laugh*.) Spoilt boy is hungry, I make him wait.

TWITCH. He lays me down and the pebbles dig into my back. He looks at me – Twitch, remember, please remember – strap yourself down, hold yourself back – never cut the kite string, never take your feet off the pedals, never let go of the balloon.

JACKS. There is a mirror, on the ceiling. I watch me. There's this tiny bit of flat brown skin, hairless, shining, where my neon knickers meet my thigh. I look hot. I feel invincible.

TWITCH. He's above me and I feel like I exist entirely in the two inches of clear space between his face and mine.

JACKS. I give him the green light. (*Laughs*.) It looks like a movie, my brown legs are wrapped around his white arse.

TWITCH. This will be the last time, that this will be the last time. I –

JACKS. – can hardly –

TWITCH. – breathe –

JACKS. – with the thrill of fucking someone –

TWITCH. –with the horror of sleeping with someone –

JACKS. – when you know –

TWITCH. – when you know –

JACKS. – that you will never see them again.

TWITCH. – that you will never see them again. (*Beat*.) I know he is going. I know he is going.

TWITCH *and* JACKS *freeze. Snap to memory light.*

Eighteen

Memory Four.

POLO *walks into the scene as set in Scene Seventeen.*

POLO. Nathan Harvey, university. No place for someone with a
heart like Twitch's. There was no fresher fresher; she was a
certified first-timer. Nathan, poor schmuck, had no idea what
he was unlocking. He didn't just fuck her either; he told her
that he loved her. What was a twenty-year-old boy doing
with a word like that on his lips? Two months later – on her
knees, eye against the keyhole, start to finish, Twitch
watched Nathan pump some bendy cheerleading skank.

BILLY *moves his hands in front of his crotch as if having
sex.*

TWITCH *kneels, makes a keyhole from her hand and presses
her eye against it.*

She got a shiner from how hard she'd pushed her eye against
the keyhole.

TWITCH *pushes her face against her hand painfully hard.*

Lovely Nathan ran himself a bath after, wash down, cool off,
scrub up. I've always been told that you should test it with
your toe but Nathan was one for jumping straight in. The
sole of his right foot: scalded, scarred, third-degree. Freak
accident, should have tested it with his toe, no one knows
how it happened – but Nathan Harvey never walked the
same again.

POLO *exits.* BILLY *exits.*

TWITCH *and* JACKS *remain on stage.*

Nineteen

We snap back into the set-up for Scene Seventeen.

TWITCH *stands, suddenly – she gasps.*

TWITCH. In one moment of wild idiocy I allow myself to forget what I know, I jump and whilst I'm falling I imagine a world where there need not be an end to everything.

JACKS. He comes. He's done. He zips himself up. He asks for my number.

TWITCH. And it feels like love.

JACKS *steps out towards* TWITCH. *They stop talking to the audience and begin talking to each other.*

JACKS. No. I say no. He calls – we fuck – we date – even if we fall? (*Laughs.*) Best-case scenario is you end up staring at the same cock for fifty years knowing that the man you wake up next to definitely doesn't think about you when he wanks.

TWITCH. When am I allowed to begin believing in for –

JACKS. Never being new or exciting ever again.

TWITCH. I imagine a world where there need not be an end to everything.

JACKS. I wasn't the first, I won't be the last.

TWITCH. I once heard that each lover is like a fingerprint – totally unique.

JACKS. I think of all the girls he has fucked before me and all the girls he'll fuck after me.

TWITCH. Like a fingerprint.

JACKS. I think of all the girls he has fucked before me and all the girls he'll fuck after me

TWITCH. I want to be indelible.

JACKS. I think of all the girls he has fucked before me and all the girls he'll fuck after me and it makes me feel free.

TWITCH. I don't want to be forgotten.

TWITCH *goes to get her guitar, lights rise and we slip into Scene Twenty.*

Twenty

TWITCH *stands centre stage – she begins to play 'One Thousand Miles', an original song by Gwendolen Chatfield.* POLO *looks on.*

TWITCH.
>What was there is no more
>So alive when I called
>Please give me time
>One thousand miles across the seas I'll ride
>We'll waltz on glass
>Hand in hand this moment it's our last
>It's our last, it's our last, it's our last...

POLO *enters.* TWITCH *continues to play the melody but ceases to sing. She stares at* POLO *whilst he addresses the audience.*

POLO. What was I meant to do? She was my sister, my twin, my tally-man. I didn't tell a soul. Silent sibling. Each time she fell – I would know what was coming – she dredged herself, turned herself inside out, she just couldn't shoulder it and with each boy it got worse. There was only so much I could stomach. So I left.

POLO *turns away from* TWITCH, *she sings, angry now, at* POLO's *back.* POLO, *pained, does not turn around.*

TWITCH.
>Cityscape bright lights
>Empty room lonely nights
>There's a voice in my head
>Pulls my hair shares my bed
>Please give me time
>One thousand miles across the seas I'll ride
>We'll waltz on glass
>Hand in hand this moment it's our last
>It's our last, it's our last, it's our last…

POLO retreats. TWITCH *turns to* BILLY *who sits, frozen. She sings with romantic glee.*

>Never spoke at the start
>Instead of words we used hearts
>And our eyes and fingertips
>And our hands and our lips
>Please give me time
>One thousand miles across the seas I'll ride
>We'll waltz on glass
>Hand in hand this moment it's our last
>It's our last, it's our last, it's our last…

POLO. Twitch?

TWITCH *continues to play, louder now, trying to drown* POLO *out.*

Twitch!

TWITCH *continues to play, louder still.*

Twitch!

TWITCH *stops suddenly.*

Twenty-One

TWITCH, *having removed her guitar, stands opposite her brother. They stand in silence for some time. They are between the beach and the club.*

TWITCH. I want to go for a swim with Billy.

POLO. It's gone midnight.

Beat.

TWITCH. He's leaving, Polo.

POLO. Yes.

TWITCH. You should be dancing, it's our birthday. You should be dancing.

POLO. Twitch, he's leaving.

TWITCH. I'm going to take him swimming, it will be amazing – at night, when it's warm and the sand's between your toes and it's all black –

POLO. Twitch.

TWITCH. I love him.

POLO. Don't.

Beat.

TWITCH. I don't think I can bear it.

POLO. I don't suppose you can.

TWITCH. If he forgets me, I'll disappear.

POLO. He won't.

TWITCH. They always do.

POLO. No. They don't, they never –

TWITCH. He will, of course he will, he has to, I just… I want to pin it down to make it stick.

POLO. Twitch – I –

TWITCH. Please make him stay.

Long pause.

POLO *and* TWITCH *exit.*

Twenty-Two

Back in the club. 'In for the Kill' by La Roux plays, the base is turned up much higher than the melody, it throbs through the floor. POLO *stands at the bar; he sees something in the middle distance, he's transfixed by it.* JACKS *enters.*

JACKS. Polo! Polo!

POLO (*quietly*). Yes.

JACKS. There you fucking are – where d'you get to? You missed it, his face, Polo – he looked like he was going pee himself. 'Can I have your number?' 'No.' Aw, it was brilliant! You want a drink – I want a drink – I'll get drinks –

POLO. Jacks?

JACKS. One second.

POLO. Jacks?

JACKS. What?

POLO. Look.

JACKS. What?

POLO. There.

JACKS. Where?

POLO. In the corner – by the toilets.

JACKS. I can't see anything; it's too dark – what is it?

JACKS *makes to go and investigate.*

POLO (*stops her*). Don't.

JACKS. What the fuck is it?

POLO. She's giving him head.

JACKS (*lurches forwards to look*). Aww – that is cheeky, man! Not even in the – how can you see that? I can't see anything – it's too dark – you're making it up, Polo.

POLO. I'm not.

JACKS. Drinks, let's get drinks –

POLO. Jacks?

JACKS. Stop looking, Polo.

POLO. Jacks?

JACKS. Polo, it's pervy, alright, stop looking.

POLO. I can't quite see her but he's –

JACKS. Polo?

POLO. You can see his hair, it's silver.

JACKS. Fuck off!

JACKS *looks.*

Very long pause. JACKS *steps slowly back, she looks away.*

POLO. I'm sorry – I –

Beat.

JACKS. Fuck.

Beat.

POLO. They've stopped.

JACKS. Polo?

POLO. She's getting up. I can't see her face, it's too dark –

JACKS. Don't.

POLO. I think one of her knees is bleeding.

JACKS tries to drag him round.

Your dad's smiling… She doesn't look like she's one for washing up.

JACKS. Stop it.

POLO. He's got it made.

JACKS. Polo?

POLO. I'm going to find Twitch.

POLO exits. JACKS slowly looks up.

JACKS. There's a trickle of blood running right the way down the front of her leg. Dad's licking the corner of a napkin, bends down and wipes her knee. She must have been kneeling on some glass or something. Never seen her before, not from the island, one of those wonky hairdo's – they do 'em at the salons in Pompey – I was meant to go on a course but they never sent – m–

Long pause. JACKS looks up, cautiously.

She's walking like everyone's looking but not a single head turns. Her flesh is swinging from her arms, you can see the veins in her legs, the lines round her eyes, the folds on her neck – no one fucking looks – it's like she's invisible.

Beat.

Mum always says you can't afford to have bare legs after thirty. Mum says he'll still be hers, whatever happens. Doesn't matter how long it is or who he's with – says she'll always be his wife and he'll always be her husband. She says there's honour in it. She's a mug, my mum.

JACKS exits. The music continues. It gets louder, the base gets stronger.

Twenty-Three

The beach. POLO *enters, he walks slowly, almost dazed.* POLO *traces the tide line as he walks.*

POLO. When I was away I would go walking at night, through the city. The neon stung the dark and you couldn't see a star if you tried. You see, everyone wanted Polo at their party, everyone.

Always the last to leave – barely able to stand, I would just walk; I would walk and walk, no idea where I was going. Past strip clubs, and stag parties and twinks being touched by greying men, past drunks and dykes and whores and poofs and little girls in gutters with their skirts up round their armpits. It seemed like the whole world was walking home alone. And nobody was surprised to see me there.

POLO *stands, he stares, the music continues.*

Twenty-Four

TWITCH *bursts onto the stage. She is dragging* BILLY, *hard, he is laughing but having to strain to slow her down.* POLO *remains on stage,* BILLY *and* TWITCH *cannot see him.* POLO *watches. We hear the sound of the sea.*

TWITCH. Let's go swimming!

BILLY. What?

TWITCH. The sea – it's beautiful. Two moons – you can see the reflection so clearly. We should swim out and touch the moon!

BILLY. You're mad. It's freezing!

TWITCH. It's fine – come on!

BILLY. Twitch!

TWITCH. Come on – take your clothes off!

BILLY. I've only just put them back on.

TWITCH. At night, like this – you wave your arm through the water, all the algae lights up, it's phosphorescent, it glows. It's magic.

BILLY. Twitch.

TWITCH. Please.

BILLY. You're crazy.

TWITCH. Please, it's my birthday.

BILLY. Don't try that – you little –

TWITCH (*backs towards the sea*). Please, it will be a brilliant birthday memory.

BILLY (*follows, seduced*). You –

TWITCH *and* BILLY *kiss.* POLO *watches,* BILLY *and* TWITCH *do not see him.* TWITCH *drags* BILLY *into the sea.*

Twenty-Five

'In for the Kill' by La Roux is reintroduced and thumps beneath the scene.

POLO. I'd walk and walk – and I'd try and find some quiet and I'd always end up at the river. There was a jetty, with an old party boat tied up on it. I'd walk down to the edge, get down on my hands and knees and put my ear against the beaten wood. I could hear the waves slapping against the struts, the black water gulping beneath me. I'd lean over and put a single finger in the water. She walks at night, she likes to paddle, to sit and watch the sea go out, knowing that it will always come back in. I knew, somehow, that if I was touching the water here and she was there then somehow we were in the same soup. Somehow, I was near her, we were under the same moon, part of the same sea.

POLO *exits, running. The music crescendos to an almost unbearable level then cuts.*

Twenty-Six

The beach, gone midnight, it's almost black. Through silence we hear faint singing. TWITCH *enters, slowly, singing 'She Said' by Plan B in whispers. She is soaking wet.*

TWITCH *sees something offstage, the singing stops, suddenly – she stands.*

TWITCH. Polo?

POLO *enters, also drenched. He approaches* TWITCH, *she takes a step back. He stops.*

Long pause.

POLO. There was only one heart between us and I couldn't see it go to waste like that.

TWITCH (*barely audible*). Polo?

POLO. People never think about it, really. But it's the longest relationship you'll ever have. Together, you outlive your parents and you know each other for years before you ever meet your husband or your wife. You know your brother, your sister for longer than you know your own children; for ever.

TWITCH. Polo.

POLO. Everything else is so temporary, fleeting barely lasts at all, and who can bear to be forgotten?

TWITCH. No.

POLO. You want something you can hold on to.

TWITCH *bends down to the sea edge. Lights dim to almost black*. POLO *looks on*.

TWITCH. His eyes are still, in the dark all their colour has gone. The moon reflects in a single spot in each one, like someone's frozen stars into the middle of marbles. I slide my hand into his palm and it's cold. There is a moment, a single second, less than – when the tide stops coming in and before it starts to go out. A fraction of a second when the sea stays still – the top of the tide, the top of the curve – and I always want to hold it; to press pause, to make it last. But flood tide always turns to ebb tide; the last wave coming in always turns around and becomes the first wave to go out. You can't stop it. That one wave, lifts his other arm up and off the pebbles and lays it down again. It looks like half his body is dancing. I can't move him, he's too heavy, it's like he's full of sand. I lay my head on his chest and I can hear the stones moving beneath him. I put my ear to his lips but the only thing moving is the sea.

Beat.

POLO. Happy birthday, Twitch.

TWITCH. Happy birthday, Polo.

Beat.

Polo Calvino was not looking to be loved.

POLO. Looking? No there was no need to look. I'd found her. They gave her my heart at birth.

TWITCH. Never let it go.

POLO. Indelible.

TWITCH. Mayday, mayday.

POLO. We've found a – off the coast of –

TWITCH. The sea, it comes in from every angle – it keeps us calm, it holds us tight, it tucks us in.

POLO. The great adventures of –

TWITCH. Lifeboat men, trying to save boys that thought they were bigger than the waves.

POLO. She used to say –

TWITCH. The island would sink with all those stories.

POLO. Like the one they used to tell.

TWITCH. About Polo and me.

POLO *steps towards* TWITCH, *she steps back. A pause, she walks slowly over to him, they hold each other. This is the first time they have touched.*

The End.